FAMILY OF LOVE

FAMILY OF LOVE

An Inspirational True Story of Faith and Determination

Christine F. Carpenter

CHAPEL HILL
PRESS, INC.

"The Lord is my shepherd; I shall not want."
PSALMS 23:1

*A portion of the net profits from sales of this book will be donated to
The Community Foundation of Greater Johnstown to support
continuation of its local revitalization efforts.*

ISBN 978-1-59715-104-7
Library of Congress Catalog Number 2014943391

First Printing

To Len, who loved Emily
with all his heart

ACKNOWLEDGMENTS

It has been a heavenly experience sharing a love for writing and storytelling with Kecia Bal, my friend and confidant. God is the divine connection between us. He placed us together for our journey of truth, to share His love with this generation.

I am blessed, and so grateful to God for her.

Thank you to God, the lover of my soul, for his 3:00 a.m. wake-up calls so we can write together.

Thanks to Emily and Len for sharing their amazing love story with the world.

Thank you to my husband, Joe, for his everlasting love and support; to my children Joe, Lauren, Alyse, and Christiana, and my seven sisters and two brothers; and to all my family for their constant love and encouragement to finish this undertaking.

Edwina Woodbury of Chapel Hill Press, for your love, expertise, and guidance to deliver our baby, thank you, my friend.

Shout out to Beth Shoff's fourth-grade class at Westmont Hilltop Elementary School for their energy that pushed me to write this book. Special thanks to Lexi Albert for her phone call and sweet question: "Mrs. Carpenter, is your book finished yet? I want to read it!"

Thanks, Clearwater Beach, for the gorgeous scenery to inspire my flow.

God bless everyone who reads this book. Take what you need for your personal growth and inspiration to fulfill your own dreams.

PROLOGUE

JUNE 1940 Emily's eyes, already stinging from chlorine, watered as she clasped her bag with her sewing kit, summer dresses, pajamas, and a well-worn swimsuit.

Mary Agnes wrapped an arm around her shoulder.

"It's you I'll miss most," Emily said, leaning her head against her older sister's shoulder. "I wish you were home again."

The sisters were quiet for a moment.

"Well, I wish so, too," Mary Agnes finally spoke. "But I have opportunities here, I suppose. I'm learning how a business runs anyway. And the place isn't so shabby, right?"

She gestured at the finery around her—elegant touches of lace, real satin curtains—décor the girls knew their parents couldn't afford.

"The work is sometimes tiresome. Keeping books all day, it's not the same as being a schoolgirl. Enjoy it, Emily, while you can. Helping Mum keep up the house isn't all that bad. At least you have your friends and school. It's not all work for you yet. I know you'll take good care of Mum, help her as much as you can. With me gone for so long, you've become the eldest. But you were always the most useful, sewing your dresses and suits and making everything Mum and Pop can't buy, making the most of everything.

"You've got the spirit to get through times like these. Me, I just want to be carefree again. I haven't known that since I was thirteen. It's got to get better, though, right, Sis? This Depression can't last forever."

Mary Agnes put a hand on each of her sister's shoulders. The girls shared

1

similar facial features, expressive hazel eyes and full cheeks, but the older girl was becoming a woman. It showed in her shape, the depth of her voice. The younger was still a girl, with an innocence about her, a straighter and smaller version of her sibling.

"I hope to be home soon, Emily."

She looked right at her younger sister's face.

"Sis, you look so glum. What do you say we dance before we go?"

Mary Agnes squeezed her sister's hand and walked her from a bedroom and through a hall to a well-appointed sitting room. She bent over a radio, turning the dial back and forth until she came across a melody. Glenn Miller's big band played "Blue Orchids." The smooth voice drenched the room: *I dreamed of two blue orchids so rare and full of life.*

The older girl started to sway, but Emily, playing at pouting, stood firmly.

"Em, come on. I'll be back to visit this fall, Christmas at the very latest, Mum said. I can't stand to see you without that beautiful smile. Give me that million-dollar smile. I have never, ever seen you frown."

Mary Agnes put her hands on her hips and made a face.

Emily cracked and let out a giggle.

"There we go. Much better."

Mary Agnes whispered, "Quick, before Aunt Elsie comes."

The girls made circles around the living room and then collapsed on a velvet settee, laughing.

"That couch is for company only." Aunt Elsie lingered on the last word, *only*, and stretched it out. Her shrill voice silenced the girls' laughter and the song ended, right on cue, but then a riot of applause followed, blaring from the radio. The woman shut off the wooden console with a snap and stood in front of them with her bony arms crossed.

"Come now. Stand up. The car is ready. It's back to reality for the both of you. Emilia, you have a place at your home, and Mary Agnes, the shop needs your full attention. You've both had vacation enough, I'd say. You can bid your farewells on the way.

"There's quite a crowd gathered. It's like buzzards every time we pull out the Chevrolet. Would you believe some of the neighbors asked whether they could sit inside? It's exhausting sometimes being watched around the clock just because you've got your business in order. Mary Agnes, you'll understand what I mean one day. You are quite a whiz with the books, when you focus, that is. I think we've almost got you right in shape."

Both girls were sullen now, but the summer sun shook their moods as soon as they stepped out onto the porch.

Emily did like driving, and it's true, some of the girls she knew had never been inside an automobile. The motion would lull her to sleep quickly if she put her head on Grandma's lap, but for a while she could watch the world spin and swerve and dip from her window while she sat upright.

The farewells were efficient, just as Aunt Elsie would have them. A few neighbor girls had come for the send-off. Emily struck up kinships wherever she went. She spoke a kind word specific to each of them.

"Until next summer," Emily said after she'd kissed both cheeks of the last of four girls who had come. The girls waved good-bye.

Uncle Joe scooped up and hugged six-year-old Vivienne, shiny hair neatly parted down the middle and held in two ribbons as Aunt Elsie had instructed Mary Agnes to do. He pecked Aunt Elsie's cheek and gave a warning after a quick hug to each of the girls.

"Please drive carefully." He turned to Emily once more. "Little sweet Emily, we'll see you again."

"Thank you, Uncle Joe, for having me." Emily gave him a light kiss on the cheek. "I love being here."

He helped Grandma Hvizdos and Viv, toddling in her pastel-green, freshly pressed dress and knickers, into the backseat. Emily followed in the back behind Viv, who already was asking Mary Agnes in front for an apple.

Aunt Elsie nodded to her husband. She took her place in the passenger's seat, and Mary Agnes started the engine.

Emily, sitting behind Mary Agnes, was the only one who turned to wave to the girls and relatives standing near the house—erected with the finest Italian-imported cut stone and the most stately on Belmont Street.

Despite all her chilly mannerisms and strictly enforced rules, Aunt Elsie was generous with her nieces in a way. She had brought Mary Agnes in to help with baby Viv six years ago, and the thirteen-year-old girl had taken to keeping the books like a regular hired accountant. She dressed and cared for the baby and helped Aunt Elsie prepare when guests were expected for dinner parties. The girls knew she loved them, or at least could be counted on to help them. Maybe that was love, in a way.

Emily wished her summer trip could last longer than two quick weeks. She could forget the tedium of housekeeping and play with her sister like they used to do at home with Mum and Pop, before everyone started to struggle so hard for money. Those in the Slovak side of town (all Emily really knew anyway) who didn't struggle feared they would. They all worked relentlessly with whatever they could find, trying to frighten away poverty with sheer muscle. It was as if the perceived virtue of scrubbing and ironing and planting without stopping would beat away the bad in the world—the Depression or talk of war against the Germans or Japanese.

Aunt Elsie had found a way to make it. She and Joe built their hardware store from a horse stable in Johnstown's Moxham area and lived upstairs until the shop swarmed with local U.S. Steel mill workers. They came for supplies to use in their second jobs as handymen, painters, and scaffolders. Krisay's Hardware thrived while everyone else scraped what they could of money and hope, trying to make it last.

The shining automobile drove past the mills—rows of tall rectangular buildings, one after another after another, along the river. Homes, all built tall and narrow and pressed together, soon gave way to the countryside that eventually would lead them back over the Mon River and back to Canonsburg. Viv leaned against her Grandma Hvizdos's shoulder. Her long lashes eventually rested on flushed, puffy cheeks and she slept, breathing peacefully through parted lips.

The car was quiet, and Grandma Hvizdos gave Emily a smile and patted her lap with her wrinkled hands. Emily leaned over Viv's legs and felt Grandma stroke her hair until she drifted into gentle slumber. Viv's kicking woke her a while later.

"How far are we, Aunt Elsie?" Emily asked, with a yawn.

Her aunt sighed and turned toward Emily.

"I don't think it will be much longer, Emilia. Practice patience. Please straighten your hair. You can at least try to look like a girl and act like a lady."

Emily wiped perspiration from her forehead and then tucked a stray lock of blond behind her ear and rolled her window down farther. She floated her left hand into the wind and felt the swift air cool her fingers up to her forearm. Her hand glided up and down as she gazed out at green hillsides, and she soaked in the glory of summer and the glamour of riding, fast, in an automobile.

I'm fifteen, and Aunt Elsie still thinks I'm a tomboy. Well, I know someone who thinks I'm pretty and just right as I am, right now. She found herself wondering what her beau was doing at this moment and whether he'd be happy to see her return. *He'll be beside me in church tomorrow morning. Yes, there is something to look forward to at home. Mum and Pop are warming up to Len even if he is Italian and not Slovak. It was the May Crowning at St. Patrick's that really did the trick.* Len had invited her parents and baby sister, Clara, to that side of town. The children singing in harmony, the poetry— Whence comes those sounds so sweet and clear . . . They fall upon my listening ear—the guards on either side of the Blessed Mother (Len was one of them), everything down to the smallest fresh-cut flowers had delighted her parents' sense of religious decorum. They'd come back to Strabane and her Slovak neighbors singing the praises of those Italians. The next time any of the neighbors told Pop his daughter was going to get murdered on that side of town, he straightened him out. "Don't tell me nothing about those Italians. They did something so beautiful; you'd never believe their faith."

She smiled to herself and looked out at the farmland, black cows dotting expanses of green. Nothing could go wrong now that Len was in her life. She had someone to go home to, someone who cared for her.

"Emilia, please put your hand inside. If a car passes, it could take that hand right off your arm," her grandmother scolded in Slovak.

Reluctantly, Emily obeyed, even though she knew there were few cars on city roads and even fewer on highways through the country.

She'd rolled the window back up halfway when she heard it down through her bones: a scream from hell and an all-consuming sensation of screeching tires, smashing metal, and shattering glass together in an instant. It jolted through her body and then left only darkness for a time. Emily didn't know how long.

"Oh, God. My brakes went," a man's voice said, coming closer. His footsteps quickened and he started crying out to God.

"Is everyone alive? Oh, dear God. Oh, Jesus. Please, tell me everyone's alive."

Viv shrieked over and over with all her lungs.

"No, there are children. God, no!"

Emily, weeping but without tears and holding her side, reached one desperate hand past jagged steel for her sister. Fire twisted in her chest with every labored breath.

CHAPTER 1

FEBRUARY 1942 When the bell rang at seven o'clock, Emily was awake, squeezing the wooden beads of her rosary. She couldn't kneel, so she had propped herself with two pillows, her body hunched on the twin-sized bed.

The clanging startled her, rattling her thin frame, but she focused again and ignored the rustling sounds of other girls crawling out of their beds.

God, please give me strength. I'm afraid. I can't face today without you. Thank you for never leaving me.

Nurse Heidi swung wide the door to the girls' room.

"Get up already. You should be out of bed." She pointed at Emily.

She scowled and huffed and then marched over to the big windows across from the girls' beds, pushing open heavy polyester curtains. The first traces of dawn filtered in and covered the room in half light. The middle-aged woman, white shoes and thick calves grounding her muscular figure, crossed her arms and looked back at Emily, thin for age seventeen and moving slowly off the bed.

"You, too?" Nurse Heidi huffed again. "No one can do anything for herself today, I see."

The woman grabbed Emily's left elbow and helped the girl to her feet. She pulled a black floral housecoat off a wall hook.

"Breakfast is waiting for you, princess," the nurse said, tossing the robe on her bed and taking one more scornful glance at the girl before leaving the room.

Emily took her rosary and put on her robe. She moved toward a small dresser with a tiny mirror and comb on top. Gripping the rosary once more, she kissed Jesus's feet and placed it next to the mirror. Her face lacked color. Her cheeks, once fleshy and pink, seemed pale and flat against her face. She gave her golden locks a few swipes with the comb, pinched her cheeks, and then joined a line of others, walking as quickly as she could manage toward the second floor and its metal dining tables.

She sat quietly next to the girls at a table for eight. When she could silence the sounds of coughs in her mind, she almost could imagine they all were lining up for a meal at a refined boarding school for girls. It was a thought she played with sometimes to guard herself from the creeping idea, the fact, that no matter how much "chin-up" talk the doctors and nurses gave, no matter what cheerful articles were written in the newsletter, *Spunk*, the girls were expected to die, some soon. Some, no doubt, would suffer for years.

Heidi stomped over to the table.

"Edith?"

A girl, no older than seven, raised her hand without looking up through her thick glasses.

"Two eggs today. I'll be checking to see that you drink your milk, too."

Nurse Heidi went down both sides of the table with a clipboard in her left hand, pushing a cart of mostly raw eggs, fresh from the henhouse nearby on the sprawling mountain property, and milk with her right.

Emily's stomach turned at the mug of raw eggs Nurse Heidi set in front of her. The nurse glanced at her clipboard.

"Oh, princess gets pears today, too." She set pear slices on a plate wrapped in plastic in front of Emily.

Irene, a tall brunette girl sitting next to Edith, snickered.

Rose reached a hand over to Emily's and spoke softly. "We missed you yesterday at dinner. Hope you're feeling better."

A small bowl of pear pieces, charred toast, a tall glass of milk, and a cup of beaten raw eggs—it was far from the comfort of simple fresh bread and milk her mother would have served on an embroidered tablecloth from the

Old Country. Emily added a bit of milk to the eggs and tried to gulp down the slime without thinking or breathing. The pears would be reward enough. She fought the impulse to gag, set the cup down, and sipped at her milk to wash away the taste.

After breakfast, Nurse Heidi was relieved from her overnight shift. Nurse Nancy, short and spirited, watched as the girls cleared their dishes into an industrial-sized trash can and set them in a huge pan of bleach-scented water. She smiled at Emily as she passed and gave her a light pat on the back.

Walking back to her ward, Emily reminded herself to say a prayer of thanks for Nurse Nancy and her healing touch. She was the one who would take the time to smack Emily's back with two cupped hands in a rhythmic massage that would loosen the mucus. Emily had never seen Nurse Nancy do that for other patients.

She opened her dresser and held the stack of letters from family and friends and thumbed through them until she saw the card. Though he'd come to see her and other girls had pressed, Emily couldn't do more than smile when nosey girls asked about Len. She had watched them trying to eavesdrop on the telephone line when she talked to him, urging her to hurry so they could use the phone.

She heard other girls passing in the hallway, some chitchatting and others trying to muffle relentless coughing. She opened the birthday card she'd read at least a hundred times.

My One and Only Goldietop,

How is my girl? Those nurses had better be looking after you. I need you better. I need to see that pretty girl next to me at the soda shop. Everywhere I go in this town, I imagine you're right here with me again, Em, smiling and holding my hand. Please, don't give up.

I saw Red the other day. We all miss you. I stopped at your parents' house, too. We said a novena for you around your kitchen table.

I'm working with Pop at the mill every day and saving for when you come home, and I'm practicing my dance steps with Cynthia in the evenings.

I hope, with all my heart, that you are improving. It hurts me to think of you doing everything you can to be brave there, in that awful place. You know I can't wait to hold you in my arms. Em, do you remember our first kiss? I look forward to more.

You have my love forever, Len

Emily fixed the stack of letters in the dresser drawer and closed it. She covered her head with a blue scarf her mother had crocheted and tucked a rosary in her pocket before going to meet others who waited near the top of the steps.

Though it was Nurse Nancy who had arranged to allow Emily and Edith to pray at the chapel on treatment day while other girls studied, it was Nurse Margaret who met them to walk through the boys' hall downstairs and down the path toward the cottage with a cross for a steeple.

It wasn't cold for February, but the girls clutched their scarves and overcoats tightly as they walked past rows of bare maples mixed among evergreens to a bus that carried them on a narrow road through the property. It passed other grand buildings and an expanse of brown grass and melting snow. The short walk and mountain air had improved Emily's spirits. She hadn't had a coughing spell all morning.

But tuberculosis, stubborn, wouldn't be forgotten. It waited in her lungs until some hopeful thought disrupted it. Looking forward toward the Mary and Jesus statues near the altar, Emily had just begun her prayers on her knees in a back row of wooden folding chairs. The girl kneeling to Emily's right inched away as the familiar shaking took hold of Emily's torso. Emily stared through her arms at the boards of the wooden chapel floor and tried to control it. She sucked in gasps of air between barks until they extended into a long stretch of coughs that wouldn't allow breaths between. Her head struck the seat in front of her as she curled toward the floor, weeping and struggling for air, panicking for breath.

The screech of folding chairs pushing forward caught Nurse Margaret's attention and she hooked her arms under Emily's and drew her up to a seat. She gave Emily's back two firm pats to clear the mucus and handed her a cup. Through tears, Emily looked up at the simple crucifix and mouthed a wordless prayer before the coughing started again and then again.

When it quieted, Nurse Margaret took her elbow to leave.

"It's all right, Sweetheart. You can pray anywhere. God listens wherever you are," Nurse Margaret whispered as they walked outside the snow-covered chalet with Edith following behind. "You'll feel better after treatment this afternoon."

Emily held her rosary over her heart as they walked back to the bus. As they stepped through the new brick building's stone columns and passed the front desk and a visitor's area, she asked Jesus over and over for strength for what she knew awaited in the second-floor doctor's office.

Please comfort me. Please keep me and hold me. Never leave me, Lord.

She felt her heart race as they got closer to the cramped space marked "Treatment Room."

Doctor Preston didn't speak when Nurse Margaret guided Emily to a scale and then to a cold metal table in the sterile treatment room. He glanced at a notebook for a few moments as the nurses helped Emily undress down to her slip.

"Weight?"

"She's at ninety-six pounds," Nurse Margaret informed him.

Dr. Preston scratched the number with pencil on his book and then scooted on his stool toward the girl.

"Okay, Ms. Lesso."

Dr. Preston stood and looked directly and impatiently in her eyes.

"How are you feeling this week?"

He ordered her to take a deep breath.

"Well, I've just had a spell at chapel," Emily started. She realized it was the first time she'd spoken that day and her voice sounded mousier than she'd hoped. She wanted to sound strong and able, but her voice betrayed her. "My ribs are sore, and I can hardly stand any more raw eggs. I'm trying everything I can to—"

"That's just what we like to hear. Fighting spirit. You must keep trying." Dr. Preston cut her off and turned back to his notebook, then peered at X-ray films.

"Your treatment will keep you moving in the right direction, Emily. Hopefully, you'll be well enough to visit the girls' auditorium for a movie by next week. Mr. Miller said he's working on bringing in a new Randolph Scott picture. We take great care to provide our patients incentive to continue to improve. We can't help you if you don't want to be helped. But I can see that you are one of the ones who do."

But Emily only heard sounds. She couldn't process the words because she saw the six-inch needle on a steel rolling table.

The doctor ordered her to take several breaths as he listened through a stethoscope.

"Okay. Now, lie down and turn on your side, and we'll give those lungs a chance to repair themselves. You know the drill."

Nurse Margaret helped Emily turn on the hospital bed. Emily lifted her arms and put her right hand under her head and the other over her left ear, elongating her body as she was directed to do. She tried not to think about the long needle. She tried not to think about her friend, sixteen-year-old Evelyn, who, like others, had left the treatment room dead, head covered. For a while, the girls all would rush to a hallway to gape at a covered body, curled in familiar pajamas under a blanket. At first, talk would spread through the girls' wards every time a patient was lost to the risky procedure and wheeled down the hill to the facility's morgue. Not anymore. Death became a quiet but regular visitor, the empty seat at breakfast or a twin bed stripped of its sheets. Seven died a week on her floor. *Seven.* Emily fought her thoughts as she smelled iodine and felt the cool wet cloth when the doctor behind her disinfected her side and then gave a sharp warning.

"All right now. We are all ready. Let's go ahead and count down from five. Five, four . . ."

She felt the first prick and clenched her teeth. She shut her eyes tightly, prayed, and started her own counting. She was at thirty-five when she heard the doctor speak again.

"Good. I think we have the right spot.

"Now administering the gas. You've made it through the worst, Ms. Lesso. Margaret, please read the pressure."

Emily blocked out the sounds and stopped counting because it was a measure of time. At first, she spent her treatments counting the shiny white tiles on the floor. But after a year or so, she tried not to count or keep time or dates, because they moved too slowly here on this table, the treatment room, and the facility altogether. She prayed. She thought of Len, imagined they were ice skating and laughing on Willowbeach Lake, when cold air was invigorating and not damning. He'd grabbed her arm when she started falling forward, legs slipping behind her. Then he'd almost tumbled but they held each other up. When they had steadied, he'd touched her chin with a strong, gloved hand and tilted her face toward him for what was their second kiss, short but tender, just like the first long-awaited one. "You are really something, Emily. I can't even say what it is about you, but I want to give you everything. I've only seen you a few times, but that's all I need to know this for certain: I'm yours." She'd hoped it was true with everything inside her. She still hoped.

The sharp pain of the needle brought her back to the sterile treatment room.

"All finished up here, Ms. Lesso. You rest now and keep that positive outlook."

She heard the click of Dr. Preston's shoes as he strode to the other side of the room. Nurse Margaret held her left arm firmly as Emily struggled to sit up, belly swollen and pushing up against her lungs.

"Your tired lungs can recuperate now with that full belly," Margaret said, upbeat. "Let's get you to your ward so you can try to get some sleep before lunch."

Emily couldn't think of food. She leaned against Nurse Margaret as she inched, bloated, to her room. The nurse snapped shut the curtains before tucking Emily tightly in her bed, the second in a row of six. A couple other girls, Lilith and Pauline, already were tucked in, hands folded over their chests and eyes closed.

But Emily couldn't nap with a body puffed with air. She knew she shouldn't let her mind wander either.

How long had she been there? How many weekly treatments had she survived? Mum had said coming here was for the best, that sometimes God used what men designed. Sometimes, we didn't know it but He was working something. But what else could she have said? Her mother would have preferred to try herbal treatments and loving prayers to undertake Emily's care in the girls' quiet upstairs bedroom, but the family couldn't refuse sending her here. As soon as her saliva sample came back positive, the small-town doctor had broken the news in his office with a terrified glance at his nurse. Phthisis was another name he called it, and consumption. He could hardly speak the word, the sounds: TB. Emily was ordered to go. Just as soon as the state could send a car and make room at the facility, she had to go. She was condemned. As Emily left with her mother that day, she'd heard the doctor directing his nurses to wipe down everything in the reception area, that it had to be disinfected, that it could be "contaminated."

For weeks, they waited until there was space at the facility. Her mother had mixed teas and salves from dried garden herbs and prayed—with enough fervor to make her brow drip with sweat—at her feet for Mary to deliver her sweet baby girl. That was one of the only times Emily can remember her father in her small bedroom that overlooked the rows of cabbage, zucchini, and potato in her backyard. He gave her what no one else could: love without pity. She held onto his words as tightly as he had embraced her that day. "Emily, you can do this. This is how little girls are made strong. We all have to go through something in life. This is your something. You will make it through, Emilia."

Then there was the car ride with the lanky driver hired by the state who said practically nothing the entire four-hour drive, even when Emily's father tried to ask him about the others who had been transported. "Did all the children have to be sent away?" he had asked. The driver had only shrugged, expressionless. His silence said everything. It was the first time Emily had been in a car since the truck lost its brakes and slammed right where she was sitting on the car ride back from Aunt Elsie's. Emily knew, that day, that something was wrong. She felt a broken rib's piercing pain. The doctor, who had refused to see her then without insurance, rushed to test her sputum when it seemed she was a "public health risk." That crash likely made way for the tuberculosis or aggravated bacteria already festering. That's what the doctor guessed anyway. No one really knew enough about this disease that didn't discriminate by class or era. All they knew for sure was fear.

Though her parents tried to reassure Emily, they couldn't mask their helplessness. Uncertainty showed in their eyes and through the subtle wavering in their voices on the way to the facility. In the backseat, Mrs. Lesso had whispered prayers and patted Emily's back. The gaunt teenager rested her head on her mother's lap when she could, in between vomiting into a bag sent by the doctors and wiping the edges of her mouth and forehead with a damp compress. Len was there next to her on that ride, a seemingly endless procession drenched in the stench of vomit, blood, and mucus in close quarters. Emily remembered telling everyone in the car, "I'm so sorry." Len wanted to comfort her, but no one knew what to say or expect. *What else could they do? The doctors said they had to send her away.*

They wondered at the winding roads through the woods that led, without warning, to a great expanse of manicured lawns. Hidden atop this isolated Pennsylvania mountain, they were surprised to find a series of enormous brick edifices, carefully arranged like an Ivy League campus. They had to hope against what the doctor had said but didn't know how. Len brushed her hair with his fingers before he carried her in to a waiting wheelchair. In the midst of swift but efficient admissions procedures, Nurse Nancy had urged the administrators to let Emily keep her hair long upon arrival. She was one of the clean ones, not one of the impoverished city children, Nancy had said. *Thank you, my angel, Nurse Nancy.*

Len always said he loved her hair.

She had lip-read the words, "Goldietop, I love you," as she'd waved to him from a balcony that first day, the day she lost her girlhood. That was the day she knew she had to pretend to be brave in the face of something she didn't understand. Even the doctors didn't understand how to defeat this ruthless plague, and so they sent her here.

On the stand next to her bed, she saw the note Len brought for her sixteenth birthday last fall, with two pressed roses. Without trying, she measured the days. Yes, her birthday had passed again. Christmas had come and gone, again, with the evergreen the girls had hung plastic birds around. That must have been two months ago. Her Christmas prayer was that she'd be home by now. For a full year—all of age sixteen—and four months, she had spent every monotonous day inside these bare walls, lining up for prescribed foods in the cafeteria, laying prostrate for treatment in a white-tiled room, or practicing schoolwork in a regimented classroom. Every night at the nine o'clock bell, she was ordered to sleep in her sparse twin bed at the preventatorium.

CHAPTER 2

The treatment stifled Emily's urge to cough for four days. The girl was just starting to lose the feel of a balloon when she felt the familiar scraping sensation as she inhaled. She could sense the stickiness in her lungs and dreaded the coughing attacks she knew would follow. The bruise from the last treatment's needle had not even healed yet.

Watching the next shift of nurses march down a snowy hill in military-style rows, Emily was sipping her milk from the wagon that came around every morning when the first series of coughs hit and made her spew the thick mix of milk and mucus. Bernice, standing next to her, gave her back some gruff pats. Emily curled away from the sturdy girl. Nurse Heidi grabbed Emily by the arm and pulled her a few steps backward.

"Didn't keep down your milk again, I see," she said. "You know, eating is your duty now. It's the only way you'll improve. Bernie, I know *how* you care for Ms. Emily, but you must not touch a patient when she's coughing out contaminated air and milk."

Bernie, husky and awkward like a boy reaching adolescence, dropped her shoulders. She gave Emily a compassionate look.

Emily tried to nod, but the spell had overtaken her body.

"Just go to your room, please," Heidi ordered.

Emily stumbled back toward her room, coughing into an arm. In the hallway, she spotted Nurse Nancy in Mary's old room, the one where Bernice slept, spraying down curtains.

"Oh, dear Emily, you've only just had a treatment."

Nurse Nancy turned toward the frail girl, gently guiding Emily to bed. She stood behind the teenage girl and gave strong pats—one, two, three—to clear her chest. Emily spit putrid green into a cup and threw it into a waste bin.

"You've had a rough go of it, Emily. All this time here. I'd hoped to see you better by now. You've such a giving heart. I know there's a purpose for you. I know you'll make it through."

Emily's spirit sagged, and it showed in her eyes. The smile she was known for, the one that could brighten a room, had been missing for days. The nurse gripped the fatigued girl's face, wiping tears from her cheeks.

"You're always so friendly. I'd say you're one of the most popular girls we've had here. Those youngsters really love you. You're the only older girl who's ever given them time. I imagine they look at you as an older sister, the way you care enough to listen to their chatter. You have a gift, Emily. You're needed, and you can't give up. Please, don't give up.

"Besides, I've got something to cheer you."

The nurse stood in front of Emily now. She was so short that she and Emily were eye-to-eye even when the girl slumped on her bed.

"There's a new girl, all full of moxie like you've always been. I think you'll find in her a kindred spirit. Her name is Frances. She's getting washed up and admitted right now. I think the two of you will get along famously. You rest and I'll introduce you this afternoon."

Emily woke to Nurse Nancy gently touching her foot.

"Mail, dear. You've got something good this time, plus a letter. I told you things were looking up. I've told Frances—oh, but she calls herself Frankie—all about you. She's excited to meet you soon, maybe in the cafeteria today."

"Thank you, Nancy, for all your kindness."

Emily brightened, especially seeing a gift trimmed with gold ribbon. But this wasn't marked from the sanatorium post office.

The girl turned the package in her hands and sat back down on her bed. She placed a letter from Mary Agnes on her bed stand. The package was about six inches square. Emily carefully unwrapped the paper, opened a box, and pulled out a note and a painted porcelain cat. She recognized it from the craft shop where healthier girls spent time doing leatherwork or painting vases and ceramic animal shapes. She unfolded the slip of paper.

Emily, I made this for you. I'm hoping you feel better this afternoon. I need to see you.

It was signed, "With much love, Bernice."

How thoughtful. Emily put the painted cat with green slanted eyes and tulle embellished collar under her bed, next to a porcelain horse Bernie had painted white and given her three weeks ago.

Now, to the letter from Mary Agnes. Heart racing, Emily reached for her letter opener, eager to hear news from home.

> To My Sweet Sis, Emily,
>
> How much I miss you! Summer will be here soon, and perhaps you'll be well enough to come back for summer vacation again. I think I may be busy, but you can help me get settled. I've something to tell you. I'm afraid to say it. I wish things could be as they were before the crash, but I guess everything changes. Have you heard from Mum?
>
> Okay, I have news I just can't keep from you any longer. Jacob has asked me to marry him! Yes! Finally someone bold enough to ask, and I do think I love him. Can you imagine, me a wife with my own house! Elsie's place is fine, but I'll have my very own home and my own husband to love and care for me! I'll have my own parties to throw instead of planning for Elsie. I will be dressing my own daughter instead of Viv.

A tightness found its way to Emily's heart. This time, it was a deep knot of heartache, not the disease that squeezed at her chest. She had always known Mary Agnes would marry. The boys never stopped staring any time she was around, always dancing, her green eyes sparkling when she laughed.

Mary Agnes was sweet and pretended not to notice the attention. It wasn't jealousy Emily felt, but longing. Len was faithful to visit her, even daring to kiss her on the rooftop in her contagious condition. During those intimate, rooftop talks and wistful letters, their love grew, but so did the bacteria inside. Would they ever be husband and wife, the parents of lovely girls in pigtails? *A girl's dream*, she thought. She kept reading.

> I have to tell you all about how he asked me. It's so romantic. I can hardly believe it's my own life. Oh, my only concern, Sis, is that you aren't here to share it with me. I've dreamed my whole life about my wedding day, and I always picture you as the maid of honor, holding my train. Remember that dress you made? I picture you wearing it and standing right beside me in the church. I thought of waiting, but Jacob won't hear of that.
>
> Oh, but I need you with me. I need you to be part of this, Em. But I've come up with a solution for that: We're going to come see you. I told Jacob that we absolutely must. We are stopping, I think, on the way to New York for our honeymoon. I can't wait until you see my lace gown. It's all happening so quickly after all this waiting. I've been afraid to tell you. It seems so wrong without you. Please, please don't be upset with me and try to understand. I love you dearly, but I can't delay this. I'm going to be a wife! It's true. I can hardly believe it. I need you to be happy for me, Sis, please?
>
> Love you with all my heart,
Your older sister Mary Agnes
(The future Mrs. Jacob Respet)

Tears escaped and slipped down her cheeks as she folded the letter and placed it neatly into its envelope.

I won't be my sister's maid of honor. I'll miss her wedding day. This disease has severed me from my own family. These moments are slipping by—gone forever, without me.

Emily thought of the three girls of whom she was the middle. She remembered home before the Depression took Mary Agnes to Aunt Elsie's and before TB locked her away. After the girls finally had finished with the day's chores, they'd sit together in Mary Agnes's bedroom and tie their hair up in rag curls. They'd giggle about the day and they'd sing "Awake in a Dream" or "Gee, You're Swell" or any popular song from the movies that Mary Agnes had heard in school. They'd stretch across the bed, dreaming about weddings, lace gowns, veils, and bouquets of fresh flowers as big as your head. They would be ravishing, walking with their father toward a handsome and faithful husband at the altar. *Was that really my life?* It was a dream world, or it seemed that way now.

Next were prayers, first as a family in the living room with all of them on their knees, hands folded. Lit candles carried heartfelt prayers to heaven. They each faced toward the Virgin Mary on a doily-covered table, and then there were individual bedside prayers.

After an early-morning breakfast of fresh bread, milk, and baked eggs with garden veggies, and then starching and ironing, Mary Agnes, Emily, and then baby Clara (when she was old enough) walked two miles to church every morning, no mind to the weather. It was all work, but they were so happy. Emily could do anything for herself—she'd helped delivered her first baby, a light-haired boy named John Mark, when she was just eleven. Now she barely could make it through a meal without fatigue or a fit of coughs that meant she had to return to bed—and now she would be isolated while her sister married. Yes, everything was changing. Never would she be that girl in her room sewing knee-length, pleated skirts fitted for her friends. *Will I ever be anything but an invalid? Will I ever be a bride like my sister?*

The thoughts swam through her mind and sank down, deep into her heart. For a while, the routine of the sanatorium—administrated, in part, by retired military personnel—had numbed her mind, but lately even monotony itself had worn off, and she'd grown restless. Her dread of the treatments grew each time another girl died, despite her fervent prayers. Death happened daily, to the point that none of the girls asked why a friend was missing. They knew.

⌐

"Emily, let's get you out to the porch for some sunshine. I've arranged a spot for you right next to Frankie."

Nancy helped the girl into a floor-length housecoat, another treasured gift from her parents, with wide lapels and decorated with big flowers. It was looser than Emily remembered.

"I'll tell you, Emily. I know you're going to love Frankie."

Emily eased herself onto a reclining chair and looked out at sun rays beaming off snow. Bernie, two chairs down, waved.

"You are so kind," Emily spoke. "And you're a very talented painter, too. Thanks for thinking of me. It cheered me up."

Bernie nodded. Her cropped brown hair shook.

"I always do."

Nurse Nancy was giddy when she walked down the long porch with a girl and blocked Bernie's view of Emily. The nurse was right. The freckled redheaded girl looked healthy and friendly.

"And here she is."

Nancy gestured toward Emily.

"Emily, hello. I'm Francis Eloise. Friends call me Frankie."

The girl was smartly dressed in a tweed tailored skirt and jacket.

"I'm just getting accustomed to being in this place."

Emily tried to stand, but Frankie gestured for her to stay and settled herself right next to her.

"Nancy told me a lot about you. I hope you didn't have too rough a time getting settled?" Emily gave a warm smile.

"Not so far," Frankie responded. "They've put me in a room with a girl, kind of looks like a boy, short hair, but they probably cut it all off, poor thing"

She whispered the last part after she spotted Bernie a few chairs down from Emily.

"I guess only the ones who are bad off get a place for themselves."

"You're Bernie's roommate?" Emily asked. "Oh, she's nice. You'll like her. She has a generous spirit, even if she seems a bit tough."

"Well, I'm glad I've got you to show me around instead. What I want to know is this: Where do they hide the sweets? I haven't had a piece of candy in weeks. Mum hid all of it when I got sick. Doctor said he wants me eating healthy and hearty stuff, as few carbohydrates as possible—whatever that means—and more milk than I can handle."

Emily gave a knowing look.

"I found where she stashed it, though, Mason jar under the sink. She never could handle my antics."

The girls laughed and kept laughing and whispering through the hour they were allowed on the porch. Frankie reminded Emily of Red, her schoolgirl friend from home.

"You know, you're like an angel. You're my angel here," Frankie said, standing up to go in for supper. "I felt so alone today. Emily, you sure do have a way of making me feel comfortable. In exchange, I have to show you some things from 'the outside.'" The redhead's eyes widened with the word *outside*.

"I'll sneak you candy as soon as I can get my hands on some. Oh, and the jitterbug! It's all I did with my friends when we had spare time. Do you know how yet?"

"No." Emily shook her head. "But I love to dance."

"Poor dear. You've been jailed here for too long. Never mind. You'll adore it. I'll show you tonight, okay? Promise."

Frankie's words moved quickly and kept on.

"It's simple. You'll love it. I hope you still dance here. Nancy said there's a radio to listen to at night, though it's only an hour. That's hardly enough, right? We'll let the other girls listen to the programs, and I'll show you the steps after supper. You're all right by me, Emily."

Emily smiled and nodded and Frankie kept chattering, even when Nurses Heidi and Nancy were ushering girls off the porch and to the supper table for vegetable stew. This time, Emily finished her meal. She realized how hungry she'd been, and she felt enlivened by Frankie's energy and the idea of dancing again.

"Are you sure you feel up to this?" Nancy asked.

"I feel better than I have in a while, Nurse Nancy. You were right about Frankie."

"I just knew it. Let's get you to the game room then."

Shirley Temple's sugary voice singing "Animal Crackers in My Soup" on a new radio program kept the youngest of the sick girls, some of them as small as four, entranced around the wooden radio. A few of them who looked up ran to hug Emily when she walked past. She stopped and gave each of them a tight squeeze.

"Won't you brush my hair again tonight? Please?"

It was Edith, who reminded Emily of her sister Clara when she was younger.

"Oh, yes, Edith. Go and get your brush when there's a break in the show. I want to see your drawings again, too. I hope you're still at it."

The girl nodded and bounced happily back to her seat on the floor.

"There you are," Frankie said, rushing over from an opposite corner. "You really will love this."

They strode, arm in arm, to an empty space near a window that looked out over the compound and dense winter forest.

"It would be better with music," Frankie said, flipping off her shoes. "We'll just imagine it. Okay. Start with a move to the left. Now right. Step back with your left foot."

Emily took to the moves with ease. When she looked up, the younger girls were watching her and Frankie's every move. They hadn't noticed Bernie slip in and stand firmly, arms crossed, surveying the girls from across the room.

"You've got it, Emily, easy as that. You're a natural dancer. You've got music in you."

Emily broke into a melody and Frankie harmonized. Soon the gaggle of smaller girls in nightgowns had surrounded them, each trying to mimic the dance moves and peppy tune.

Even Irene, usually wearing a bitter expression, looked up from her book to watch. A trace of a smile moved across her lips.

"What's all this?" Nurse Margaret walked in from the hallway.

"Oh, dear. Some of you—Emily, Rose—you're terribly sick. We don't want to spread anything."

The girls froze, and Margaret looked at the pouts on the little ones' faces and heard the collective sighs. Instead of breaking them up, she stepped to the radio and switched the large dial to music, a swinging dance tune. She started tapping one of her white nurse shoes and then spoke, adding an air of forced sternness to her voice.

"Just don't be reckless. Now, don't you get too close. Spread out a bit."

Edith ran and hugged Margaret's square hips. Her arms didn't quite reach all the way around, but Margaret, surprised, rubbed the girl's bony back. The hour passed quickly, and there were finally more peals of laughter than coughs in the game room.

⁀

"You are a dear, an angel," Frankie said back in Emily's room when Edith, beaming with anticipation, padded over, holding a silver brush and comb.

"Will you braid it, too, please?"

As soon as Emily nodded, Edith jumped onto the bed, took off her Coke-bottle glasses, and waited, trying not to squirm.

"You have to tell me. Is there anyone nice in the boys' hall?" Frankie asked.

"We hardly see them. I don't know."

Emily forced a wide part through Edith's tangled locks and brushed both sides straight.

"Do you have a beau back home? I have someone, but I'm not sure of him. It's so hard to know those things."

Emily looked at the child in front of her and tilted her head to the side to start a braid. She smiled over at Frankie.

"I do. You'll meet him when he comes to visit. His name is Lenny, and I am sure of him."

"Well, I need to hear more about your Lenny and how you're so sure. You'll have to tell me everything. I'm off to write to my Charles. I'll see you at breakfast, Em."

The nickname Em—that was something she'd missed hearing.

"Goodnight, Frankie."

Edith put her glasses back and peered at Emily with magnified doe eyes.

"You're the greatest," she said, holding Emily tightly around the waist a moment before scampering to her bed and curling under her covers.

A letter is a grand idea. I'll write a note to Len, Emily thought, leaning back and pulling out stationery from the stand next to her. When she turned around, the sight of Bernice standing over the end of her bed startled her.

"That dancing, it was really stunning, Emily. You really have the moves."

"You scared me. Hi, Bernice. Yes, it was fun, wasn't it?"

Silence followed.

"Thanks again for the gift, Bernie. I think I'm going to work on a letter. Just fifteen minutes until the bell rings for bed. You know the rules. Lights out."

Bernice sighed and raked her hand through her cropped hair.

"Well, all right, Emily. I just wanted to talk with you. Everyone else always wants your attention, though. It's okay, I guess. Goodnight, Emily. I love you."

"You're a dear heart. I love you, too, Bernice."

Emily sank onto her bed with a notebook in hand, but the other girl stayed. Ideas shaped in Emily's mind—she realized Bernie's intentions—and surprise played out on her features. Bernice walked swiftly toward her and leaned close to her face.

"Wait, Bernie. Wait. Stop."

Stunned, she pushed the girl back.

"I love you, Bernie, but not that way, not like that."

Bernie, wordless, slammed the door behind her. A hush fell over the room, and the other girls on their beds turned toward Emily, flipping through empty pages of her notebook to avoid curious stares.

CHAPTER 3

Rosary in hand, another day started with prayers for Emily. This time, she felt well enough to kneel next to her bed. She whispered prayers of thanks for Frankie, for Lenny and Nancy—those angels in her life. She prayed, too, for Bernice.

It must be an awful feeling. I guess we never know what our neighbors are experiencing. Let me show love to each one. Let me learn from each one and show understanding and compassion. Bless my dear family, Mum, Pop, Clara, and Mary Agnes.

It was then she remembered her sister's news, the wedding.

Be with them as they approach this milestone.

The thought of her sister in her wedding gown pricked at Emily's heart, but she kept praying. *God, bless Jake and Mary Agnes.* A few minutes later, she checked the date on the letter, written in her sister's ornate cursive. It had been written weeks ago. Mail came to the sanatorium post office more slowly than the regular post, though she didn't know why. It only had to be disinfected outbound.

Mary Agnes could be married by now.

Emily tucked the thought away and walked to breakfast. Her stomach turned at the thought of raw eggs in a cup again.

Bernice looked at the ground in the dining hall.

"Bernice—"

"Don't bother." Bernice interrupted and made a beeline to a seat at the end of the table.

Emily followed her and touched her arm.

"I'm so sorry for the misunderstanding," Emily said. "I hope I never led you to believe. . . . Do you want your gifts back?

"No, they were made for you."

"Thank you." Emily reached her arms out toward Bernie. "Can I have a hug, Bernie?"

Bernie gave a half smile and hugged Emily.

"Em, you had better save me a seat right next to you." Frankie's cheerful voice rang out from across the room.

She settled beside Emily, and Edith in her braids sat on her other side.

"Boy, was Bernie cross last night."

Emily whispered in Frankie's ear and told her about the incident, the almost kiss.

"Are you serious?" Frankie's eyes widened. "Well, that's not the kind of romance I was hoping to hear about from you, Em. I know you're charming, but, well, good grief."

"Poor thing. Imagine what that would feel like, fighting those feelings. I never thought much of it, but now I'm remembering things she said and did. Maybe it was partly my fault."

"Oh, you're kind to everybody is all. You shouldn't feel bad about that. Is that what's eating you today?"

"No, it's all cleared up, Frankie. Just still a shock to me."

"You were sparkling last night after the jitterbug. Those little ones adore you. We can practice again tonight."

Emily sighed and looked at the meal a nurse had placed in front of her—cinnamon toast and raw eggs again. She told Frankie about Mary Agnes.

"I don't know how long it's been planned, but she's to be married. I'm so far away from all of it. She could already be married. It's my own sister's wedding, and I won't be there. Maybe it's already happened and I've missed it."

Frankie was quiet. Her eyes filled with tears for her friend.

"You miss a lot in here. We've got to spring you and me out of this joint. The nurses say this treatment really makes a difference. I'm scheduled to have one soon. It does help, doesn't it? Is it scary? What's it like?"

Emily looked away and nibbled bits of her toast.

"It's a strange feeling. It's not so much about how it hurts."

She couldn't finish the thought. She didn't want to frighten her friend.

"Well, never mind those things," Frankie said. "We're going to get through this together and get back home. We'll have weddings of our own to plan one day. I wrote to Charlie, or started to. I mentioned that I have a new friend. I'll finish it this afternoon, but first I need to hear about this fella of yours."

Emily smiled for the first time that morning.

In her room that afternoon, Emily pulled an envelope of pictures hidden beneath her panties in a dresser drawer.

"He's absolutely dreamy, Em. He really is. Dark hair, pompadour, sly smile. Look at him."

Frankie dropped her body across Emily's bed lengthwise, facing toward the foot of the bed. The nurses would shriek if they saw Frankie near Emily's pillow. Frankie already had heard lectures about the tiny tubercles that needed to be avoided.

"I'm sorry, love. Tell me his name again."

The words and their cadence—Len Fenimore—Emily couldn't say them without beaming, and a hint of an Italian accent.

"Well, you're Slovak, aren't you? That's not a Slovak last name."

"No, it's Italian. Fenimore means family of love."

"And what about your family? Do your parents know?"

Emily nodded. She pulled out a photo of Len and her on a hooked, multicolor rug in the grass. Emily was sitting behind him with her arms around his shoulders.

"This was taken back home in my backyard." She held the photograph close.

"They *were* upset at first. The neighbors all said I'd get killed going to that end of town, that the Mafia was out that way. It is true they've discovered bodies. Len found one once himself. The police told him not to speak of it.

No one messes with Len, though, and I always knew that. I always feel safe with him. He's tough in one way and so gentle in others."

She told Frankie about the May Crowning with Len as a guard next to the Blessed Virgin on stage, his sister as queen, and the children all singing sweetly. It might have been the first time a Slovak family had been to the Italian Hall in Canonsburg.

"It's why I waited so long to let him kiss me. I knew Mum didn't like it, but there were other things I knew, too. I knew right away when I saw him that it was love, something that wouldn't go away. He was the handsomest guy I ever saw. Our eyes locked, and we knew that we were to be together forever."

"Well, you've first got to tell me all about this kiss."

Emily blushed.

"Please. Won't you tell me? I've never kissed a boy, or a girl, thank goodness," Frankie prodded.

"Well, we had gone on a date to the bowling alley. His buddies were there, teasing him, asking him why he was chasing 'the good girl' again. See, he'd been showing up at church, trying to talk to me. I had my reservations. I cared what my parents thought. I prayed. But he was so sweet, Frankie. He didn't give up. He knew it was right, just like I know. He just kept trying, even after his friends said to forget about me. He even punched one of the guys for making fun of him following me, that 'thing,' around."

"No way." Frankie's jaw fell.

"Oh, yes. I told you, Len has a bit of a temper. He didn't care what anybody thought, even when his dad asked why he wasn't after a good Italian girl, you know, shapely and all. He kept coming to my church and eventually I'd watch for him.

"Well, he'd been asking to take me bowling and the weather had finally cleared, so I said yes. I knew he'd have to walk five miles from his house to mine and then we'd walk a couple miles to the bowling alley and back home. We were on my front porch and it was getting late. We were swinging. I knew he was going to kiss me, but I felt kind of nervous and I think he might have been, too. He was holding my hand."

"How perfectly romantic," Frankie sighed.

"Well, that's when Mum shouted out to us."

The girls laughed.

"She must have known what was happening outside. She yelled out, 'Lenny, it's almost ten o'clock. You're going to miss that bus and be walking five miles home.' I think Lenny might have missed the bus to stay with me, but he knew Mum was trying to shoo him off. He stood up, leaned over, and gave me a strong, lingering kiss before he ran off to catch the bus."

"So did you meet him in church the first time?"

"No, I had met him before," Emily answered. "He just showed up at church to see me again." She pulled out another photo.

"That's my whole family."

From toddlers to grandparents, people packed in every space around a long cloth-covered table in the photo. There must have been at least twelve or thirteen. It was taken outside, with two big white sheets hanging over a clothesline just behind the table on the grass behind Emily's house. She could almost hear the laughter, the boisterous talk.

Emily pointed out each family member and told Frankie about the outdoor dinner parties. Family or friends always were over to visit and savor her mum's generous Slovak dishes—halupki, cabbage and potatoes, and perogies smothered in buttered onions.

That's just how I want to be someday. I want to make everyone around me feel comfortable and cared for. That's if I ever get out of here.

"I want a really big, happy family one day," Frankie spoke the same words Emily whispered in her heart and at the same time. "Did the doctors ever talk to you about avoiding pregnancy?"

Emily winced. In her daydreams, she'd live in a house with a porch full of precious kids and a church just across the street. After dinner, they'd all talk and sing together. She couldn't even picture her adult life without children to look after.

"Yes, and I won't do it. I can't imagine my life with Len without children. I want children."

"Well, you're already part way through your dream. You've found *the one*," Frankie said, sitting up. "You've met him for a reason, don't you think? Oh, you still have to tell me how you met and how you know."

"It's difficult to explain," Emily answered. She thought for a moment, but Nurse Nancy interrupted.

"You've a telephone call downstairs, Sweetie," she said. "It's your sister. You can take the call at the nurse's station."

⌒

Another nurse wiped the telephone receiver thoroughly and handed it to Emily.

"Oh, Love, did you get my letter? Please, please tell me you're not upset with me." Mary Agnes's voice trembled.

"Of course not, Sis. I love you. I want beautiful things to happen to you."

"Well, that's what I want for you, too, Sis. I didn't know it would happen like this, so quickly, just everything in a flash. I wanted you to be here sharing in all of this, too."

"It's already happened?"

"Yes, the ceremony, yes, it has."

Mary Agnes kept talking to fill up the silence. Her sister didn't speak. She didn't want to hear disappointment in her own voice. The nurse, filing papers a few feet away, gave a look of concern.

"It was lovely but not as much as it would have been with you here. I can't believe you're not through with that place. Mum worries they aren't caring for you the way she would be. You know the healer that she is."

Mary Agnes told her sister about the Slovak church, St. Stephens, the flowers, and their petite but feisty mother, overcome with joyful tears.

"You're going to see the dress, Em. I'll show you. I'll wear it there. You'll love it."

Emily swallowed hard and tried to bury sorrow.

"Yes, it's so thoughtful of you to visit. When will I see you, Love?"

"Well, I'm packing now from Aunt Elsie's. She's arranged for us to move. I'll have my own home with dinner parties. We'll move in after we visit New

York for a honeymoon. Jacob and I are coming to see you on our way. We'll be off early tomorrow morning.

"I'm going to see you tomorrow. I can't wait to kiss your beautiful face."

Surrounded by shreds of cloth, Frankie and Emily rolled their hair in rags that evening, skipping the radio program. Other girls already were resting, eyes closed and hands folded over their chests, on beds nearby. Edith had come and left Emily's bed with two long braids, ready for the spectacle the next day. All the girls were talking about Emily's visitor. They were going to see a real bride.

CHAPTER 4

"Girls! That is quite enough!"

Even Nurse Nancy, normally most patient among the caretakers, was starting to snap. Edith and Rose couldn't stop giggling over their meal of chicken soup and grain bread. Each girl at the table had taken extra care with her hair and clothes that day, most of them swooning and swirling in front of small mirrors in their rooms, daydreaming of being a glowing bride. Emily had spotted a few of them marching, pretending to hold bouquets of flowers in their tiny hands.

The youngest of them—Edith and Rose—had started kissing jokes and couldn't stop.

"When you like a boy, it's like this," Rose said, smashing the back of her hand against her mouth and batting her eyelashes. It was about the sixth time she'd done it.

"Oh, Edith. I don't know what I ever shall do if you don't say you'll marry me," Rose said in her best fake southern accent and threw her head back. It was a child version of Scarlet's voice. Many of the healthier girls had seen the first half of *Gone with the Wind* last week in the sanatorium theater, leaving them rapt in ideals of romance and puffy lace dresses. They didn't know the end. They had fallen asleep before it was over.

Edith squealed again.

Her breath didn't come back, though. The laughter sparked a coughing spell that possessed her feeble body until she was bent over the side of her chair and rocking with her arms crossed and her two braids shaking. Her face turned bright red and her eyes bulged.

"You've worked yourself into a fit, Edith." Nancy rushed over to pat her back.

"Let's get you apart from everyone else until we can get this cough under control."

The nurse turned Edith's chair around so her spit wouldn't reach the other girls. Edith's cough raged. All cringed at the sound of retching.

"Okay, dear. Let's get you cleaned up and rested so you can see Emily's sister this afternoon with the other girls."

The other girls finished their lunch in silence.

⁓

"Em, is it time yet?"

Emily felt someone giving her right arm persistent but gentle shakes. She had drifted off to sleep in the sunshine, propped up with pillows behind her on a reclining chair.

"Do you think she'll wear her veil, too?"

Edith's eyes were wide with curiosity and made wider behind her glasses.

"Sweetie, pretty soon, and I don't know if she'll wear it. I hope so." Emily still was squinting.

"I'll have the longest veil *in history* when I get married. It will trail for miles behind me when I walk down the aisle." Edith gave a great sigh.

"You will look just like a princess, Edith," Emily said, and then she nodded toward Edith's empty chair three seats down. "But you had better get back to your spot and pretend to sleep before Heidi notices you're missing."

"Okay, okay. I love you, Em."

"Sweetie, I love you, too. Go and rest."

"You have a way with those girls." Frankie was just waking, sunning herself next to Emily.

"They keep me smiling," Emily said. "So do you, Frankie. I'm glad to have a friend like you here with me."

Frankie tucked unruly red curls behind her ears.

"Well, I'm glad to have a friend like you, but I wish neither one of us were here. I have to admit, I didn't really feel so sick until I came here. I think the sanatorium makes you sick. This place makes you feel like an invalid—forced to rest, forced to eat, nurses all around, fussing at you. And I thought my mother was smothering."

"I know exactly what you mean," Emily said, with a firm nod.

"What's your ma like, Em?"

"Well, she's small but strong and spunky, too, in her way. She's always wearing heels, even cleaning up around the house. Our family started the Rosary Society in our home. She speaks to Mary like she sees her in the same room, like she's her best friend. She keeps a leather journal where she writes down her answered prayers. She taught me to pray."

"Does it help? I see you with your rosary in the mornings. My mother quit church when I was about six, right after Papa left and didn't come back. I don't remember much from that time, and I don't want to."

Emily shifted in her chair.

"I'm sorry to hear about your father. I never understood men who leave or cheat. A wedding vow is a sacred promise, to me, anyway. My pop—I love him, but I saw how much it hurt my mother when he asked another woman to dance at the band hall.

"But praying, yes, it gives you something to hold on to. It's comforting. There are times I don't know what else to do. Like you said, this place has a way of getting into your head and washing hope away. Even when you want to feel well, being here reminds you every waking moment that you're sick."

Frankie looked down. Emily reached out a hand toward her friend and whispered.

"We're going to make it out of here together, right, my friend?"

Moments later, Nancy came to tell Emily her sister was out front. The girls all stood, some with the nurses' help. Emily hooked Frankie's arm, and they pranced down the hallway together. The other girls lined up inside, waiting to see Mary Agnes.

There she was, bright green eyes welling with tears as her sister rushed to embrace her in her bridal gown.

"Even sick, you're a beauty," Mary Agnes said after releasing Emily from a long hug.

"Not like you today, Sis! You're glowing. Look at all this lace, puffed sleeves, and a string of perfect pearls all the way to your neck. It's so elegant."

"Do you really like it?" Mary Agnes turned around to show the back and all the buttons.

"It's gorgeous. Truly. Where is your veil?"

"I must have left it in the car."

"The girls, they'll want to see it. I told them you were coming, and you would have thought a movie star was going to make an appearance. They all are dying to see you."

Emily looked behind the bride to see Jacob, her groom. She welcomed him to the family with a warm hug.

"This is Frankie. She's my dear friend," Emily motioned for Frankie to step forward. She'd been leaning against a wall. Jacob nodded, then went downstairs and out to their car to fetch the veil. He returned, arms so full he had to strain to see above the frothy load.

"Here we are," Emily said, taking yards of tulle from Jacob. "Bend down a moment, Mary Agnes."

Mary Agnes sat while Emily fussed over her hair and pinned the veil with Frankie's approval until the sparkling tiara was centered perfectly and the fabric framed her face.

When Mary Agnes stood, Emily stretched and smoothed her train, the way she might have at the altar as the maid of honor during the ceremony. A group of nurses and other visitors had formed a circle around the four.

"Let's go. The girls are all waiting," Emily said, holding her sister's hand. Jacob and Frankie followed.

Girls who had been sitting stood. Their mouths dropped in awe. Mary Agnes stopped in the middle of the hall, girls all around her, petting at lace.

"You're so, so beautiful. I can't believe it," Rose said with a gasp.

"It's the prettiest dress I've ever seen." Edith squealed and looked at Mary Agnes through her glasses. "Can I please wear the veil? Can I please?"

"Of course, dear. And what's your name?"

"I'm Edith." She reached out her arms for the wisps of tulle. Emily helped arrange it on her head.

"You're lovely, Edith," Mary Agnes said. The girl twirled around until Rose asked to wear it, too. Holding a nonexistent bouquet, she marched slowly forward, keeping time with music in her mind. Four of the smallest girls had a turn before the nurses urged all of them back to their ward but Emily. Frankie smiled and waved to them, and Emily, Mary Agnes, and Jacob went to the visitors' room.

"We could go out to the veranda, but I've already spent two hours of rest time there."

"Oh, Emily, what monotony. How are you managing here for so long?"

"Just praying and waiting, I guess. Seeing the other girls, I know I can't give up."

Jacob sat next to his new wife and held her hand.

"They are something, aren't they?" Mary Agnes said. "That Edith is precious."

"I know," Emily said, with a smile. "She reminds me of Clara."

"It's hard to believe Clara is fourteen now, isn't it? Mum says she still sleeps with the doll you made her. Time moves so quickly. And now Jacob and I have our own house. Aunt Elsie gave us a pretty piece of farmland and a house, too. It was so sweet of her. And how is Len? Does he still visit?"

"Yes, every two weeks we see each other. He drives Mum and Pop and Clara out here. He's working in the mill. He's actually his dad's foreman now. His brother is serving stateside in the war. You know Len, always ready to fight. I'm afraid he wants to be drafted."

Jacob broke in. "This war is a frightening thing. If the Japanese or the Germans have their way, they'll be here bossing us around, soldiers at every street corner. We need bold fighters."

"But we need protectors here, too." Mary Agnes looked at her husband and squeezed his hand.

"I'm going to take care of you, no matter what," he said.

The three of them shared stories of home for another hour before Nurse Nancy came to get Emily to rest. She thanked them both again for going out of their way to visit, and Mary Agnes tried to give some encouragement.

"I love you dearly, Emily. Don't give up. You'll be able to go home soon. God has a plan for you. I know that for certain. You and Len will be married, too."

Emily walked them down the hallway to the staircase and then waved to them from the brick wall of the veranda until the blue Chevy, clanking soup cans and puffy paper flowers still tied on ribbons behind it, had disappeared down a forested road.

CHAPTER 5

Swaddled under blankets on a reclining chair on the terrace, Emily watched robins peck at patches of dirt swelling among melting snow two floors below. She couldn't help but sense that the blanket felt more like a straightjacket, but she tried to relax and focus on the hopping birds—spry and oblivious to the suffering within the thick brick walls so close to them. She thought of the needle going into Frankie's side: the pain and panic Emily knew so well, counting to ten and then twenty to try to stop the tears.

The birds chirped. With silent thanks, she thought of how spring would break soon. Something had to break soon. Hope couldn't be buried beneath layers of ice cold forever. It was only a season.

Feeling the strain on her neck, she let her head rest against the back of the chair, closed her eyes and tried to breathe in the cool air—finally not sharp and frigid—but her cough flared halfway through the inhale. It kept on, angry and violent, allowing only short, desperate gasps in between. She felt her ribs ache but couldn't stop the pain.

When it finally quelled, Emily noticed the break in the silence had scattered the robins.

Yes, I will tell Frankie about my sweetheart. She won't stop asking until I tell her, and I'm ready now. She had yet to really open up to anyone here about her life back home, and she and the spirited redhead had grown close over the past month. Though she hated the thought, Emily worried she was drifting away from her life—like she was imagining someone else when she remembered Len, school, her family. Even Mary Agnes was a real married woman, and it all had unfolded without her. She wanted to tell it all out loud, speak the words, speak his name, and hear her own voice tell the stories. Maybe then they would seem real again. She felt close to Frankie. Even now, her heart ached for her friend in the sterile treatment room with the doctor who didn't really see you. She whispered a prayer for Frankie to know peace.

Please, dear God, I'm asking for your help. I pray to you for Frankie right at this moment. Embrace her and all who are ill and struggling. Most of all, give her comfort and hold her. Thank you for your love. Please help her through this. Amen.

She did feel stronger, empowered to tell her story. Heart fortified, she let herself remember.

She imagined the squeak of basketballs in the St. Patrick's school gym and her friends' chatter between collective shouts and sighs of her classmates and their parents.

"Pauline is dating an older boy," her friend Elizabeth, the other Red, had said, taming the sides of her wavy ponytail. She scooted closer to Emily and their friend Mary Grace.

"He works at the mill, and he's saving up for a car. He's been walking her to school every day for the past two weeks. He gives her a kiss every time. I just know he'll drive her to prom. I know it. Maybe he'll take me and Walter, too. We could go somewhere nice before.

"Mary, has Richie asked you yet?"

Mary Grace blushed and stalled. They'd been over this talk on the walk through the snow together to the game. She took off her gray wool coat, set it on an empty seat on the bleachers behind them, and looked out at the team and then at the long-legged player with the No. 34 jersey.

"We still have a couple months until prom," Mary Grace finally answered.

"That boy is afraid to commit," Elizabeth snapped with a frown. "I wouldn't take anything like that from Walter. Richie hasn't even given you his ring yet. He's a senior. He's almost through with high school, and he still can't make up his mind to be a man. How long have you been going with him again, Mare?"

"Give her a rest, Red," Emily, sitting between them, cut in protectively. "There's no reason to fuss over prom or dates yet. I'll go with you, Mary, if he doesn't ask you, even though I'm sure he will." She reached across Mary Grace's back with her left arm and gave her a reassuring squeeze.

"We don't need anyone to drive us to prom. The whole point is to dance. We'll dance the night away."

Emily put an arm around each girl and swayed in her seat. The three girls giggled.

"What about you?" Elizabeth nudged Emily.

"What about what?" Emily gave her friend an icy glance. "I don't care. I'm not interested in Pete, if that's what you're asking. I wouldn't let him take me to prom or anywhere else. He just acts ugly. He didn't say one nice thing to me at the dance hall, and he expected me to say yes right away to a walk to the diner. He acted like I was the first girl to tell him no."

The crowd suddenly howled at the team's score, and Emily leaped from her seat with a broad smile across her face. Waves of golden hair bounced behind her.

"I'm not talking about Pete. I mean his brother, Len. I told you. The girls say he's dreamy. Wait until you see him."

Emily sat down and looked straight at her friend.

"Well, the girls say Pete's a looker, but he looks like a dog and not a friendly one, and this girl's not biting. He's just not my type. He expects everyone to jump for him. You can tell that right away, in one look."

Sometimes, one look can tell you everything you need to know.

From the corner of her eye, she spotted someone looking toward them from the back row of bleachers. She turned and their eyes locked. The game, the crowd, her girlfriends' laughter—her mind quieted everything else, like a radio program turned down low. It was noise with no meaning. All she saw, all she knew and would ever know, was him. She couldn't have described his features before they met, but she recognized the feeling she'd heard from others before but didn't think could be real: He took her breath away. She couldn't breathe, couldn't move for a moment. It was something she didn't know her heart had awaited. The longing had been there, but she hadn't sensed it before.

"Em, Em, what is it?" Mary Grace asked before turning around.

Emily was quiet for a moment. When she spoke again, her voice was calm, sure.

"The most handsome man I've ever seen."

Both girls whipped around.

"I'd be happy to introduce you," Elizabeth said, with an I-told-you-so grin. "That's Lenny. Len Fenimore."

He'd followed her to an outside hallway the moment she walked out of the game. She saw him behind her but still acted surprised when he spoke.

"What's your name?"

"Emily."

"Are you a cheerleader?"

"No," she said, looking away. "I'm just rooting for our team."

He had wanted to walk her those two and a half miles home that night, but Emily wouldn't hear of it. The snow was three feet deep, and Len, an Italian, lived clear on the other side of town, five miles away from Emily's house. Emily knew she'd see him again, and she did. Len was sitting in church the next morning when she arrived to pray with her sister.

Praying had always been her center, and now, on the sanatorium porch, she prayed again for her friend, enduring her first painful artificial pneumoperitoneum treatment to pump her diaphragm with gas and relieve her exhausted lungs. With dread, Emily remembered her next treatment was scheduled for tomorrow.

Be with Frankie. Please, Lord, be with her right now and hold her.

Nurse Margaret came outside to round up the girls who were resting. She wouldn't look at Emily but took her arm.

"What is it, Margie?"

"It's time to go in. It's getting cooler out here." The older woman still wouldn't look at Emily's face.

Inside, she walked past the room where Frankie stayed. The door was open and Nurse Nancy was over Frankie's bed, packing clothes, letters, and photos into a box.

"No, no, no," Emily screamed and ran toward the door but Margaret blocked her and gripped her arm.

"Let me go. Where is she? Where is Frankie?" She looked up, defiant, into Margaret's eyes. At that moment, she saw Nurse Heidi pushing a gurney farther down the hallway. She recognized Frankie's flannel pajamas but the girl's head was covered with a cloth.

"Come on to your room, Emily. There's nothing to be done now."

Nancy turned around, eyes red and puffy. Emily flailed, escaped Margaret's grip, and ran to Nancy and her friend's few belongings.

"When? What, the treatment? Another one? Why?" Emily sobbed, her face in her hands.

"Now, dear, we can't say why. I don't know the answer. Only God knows that." Nancy put a hand on Emily's shoulder.

"She's with the angels now. Maybe God knew this place was too small for that much spirit," Nancy said.

"This isn't how she was supposed to leave. We were supposed to get better together. Aren't any of us ever going to get better?"

"There's a plan for each of us, something each of us is to do, child," Nancy said. "He's the only one who can say when or where," Nancy's voice cracked. "But I can't say that this makes any sense to me."

Emily wept and could speak no more.

CHAPTER 6

Without words, Emily endured the next morning's treatments. It was the first time she'd ever been in that white room without praying.

Margaret coaxed her onto the scale and spoke to Dr. Preston.

"Ninety-one pounds."

"You've lost weight again, Ms. Lesso," he scolded, but Emily only looked past him with a blank, cold stare.

She went through the routine, ignoring the needle's prick. With guilt, she thought.

I don't care if they hit a vein and that's it for me. I don't care anymore. Why should I live while everyone dies around me? What kind of life is this anyway? How long can I be expected to hope while life is being stamped out around me every day?

She pushed away thoughts and the emptiness in her soul. She shut off her inner voice, hugging herself, while the doctor filled her belly with air through the needle. When she returned to her bed, the same twin bed in the same room that always smelled sanitized, she saw what had always lifted her spirits—a letter from Len. This time, she set it aside and closed her eyes.

Why did I live and Frankie die? What was it you planned for my life, God, and why would you connect me and Len, bring together two souls, only to take me away? Am I the next to go?

She wished, with all her heart, that her mother were there to care for her, to tell her what to do. Emily curled to one side, as much as she could with a swollen belly, and imagined her mother rhythmically stroking her hair until she slept.

⤙

The snow must have been two feet deep, but Emily didn't feel anything. Her feet didn't sink into the snow either. She heard it crunch beneath her, but there was no familiar sensation of stepping down, down through the cold. Inside that old familiar church's creaking doors, she was drawn immediately to the glow. There must have been a hundred candles flickering around the Blessed Mother in her shrine. Emily sank to her knees before her, lost but prayerful. She looked up at the statue. Mary's eyes seemed to look past her.

"Can you hear me? Can you hear me at all? Do you see me? Is this my fault?" Emily tried to say it, and then tried to shout it, but her voice was gone. Unable to speak, panic flashed through her. With all her might, she yelled it, "Can you see me?"

⤙

She woke startled, sweat dripping. She looked around. Edith and Pauline were sleeping, hands crossed the way she had seen dead people posed in caskets. Freezing rain rapped on the windows across the room. Months of regimented days and weekly treatments passed in the same rhythm, with no answer to Emily's plea.

CHAPTER 7

Two months and ten days after Frankie's death, the doctors ordered that Emily be moved from the Preventatorium, the facility for children, to the main sanatorium building. She'd heard, vaguely, the doctor explaining it to her and a few nurses in a meeting room after her last appointment, but it didn't register. He pointed to X-rays, talked about numbers, her weight, her treatments, diminishing lung capacities in liters. Or maybe it was just that it didn't really matter. All the wards seemed the same now, just clusters of narrow beds with metal frames and a chair for each. A place to sleep, all day, and a place to sit and wait for nothing. Even when she saw the youngest girls, who once had brought her joyous distraction, all their faces looked the same now. Children and adults in dressing gowns and pajamas. All of them on a slow march to death or a life spent hiding from it.

She spoke nothing as Nurse Nancy gathered her belongings and took her downstairs to the front desk of the facility, painted a soft, childlike mint shade to match the checkered green and white asbestos tiles on the floor. Even looking out from the front steps between mammoth columns didn't move her. The expansive lawn that once made her feel hopeful just made her feel small.

Walking toward the sanatorium building, her thoughts were dismal.

Another grand edifice in the middle of nowhere, a mausoleum, more like. An elaborate façade to distract from the vulgar business of dying.

The columns here were the same solid cut stone, three stories tall, as at the Preventatorium, only there were more here. A great, round green lawn curved around the columns. Emily walked through them without looking up. Her ward was in the women's hall on the fifth floor. When the elevator door opened, nurses in white uniforms pushed a covered body on a gurney out into the hallway toward the morgue on the first floor. Nurse Nancy hooked her arm and picked up her bag to step into the elevator after they'd left. The bellman stood aside when they reached No. 5. She saw first a door with the sign "Treatment Room" and second the sunken faces of women, slight enough to be children but with frayed, graying hair. The adults there passed up and down the pink hallways, coughing, without acknowledging anyone around them. They didn't have the fearlessness that kept girls looking around for anything good, growing, or blossoming. These women had watched their bodies deteriorate, pound by pound. They were walking death.

"We need you to rest, dear, but this much is just unhealthy." Nurse Nancy stroked Emily's hair and then set down her bag. "I know it all seems too much to handle. I wish I knew how to encourage you. You really haven't eaten like you should, and Dr. Preston is worried about your weight. I've seen a lot of girls come and go. I know there's more for you."

Cheek pressed to her pillow on a bed the same shape as the last, Emily didn't move.

"I can't see you give up like this, not you. I've seen too much here," Nancy said, standing up.

"Please, Em, think of all you have to live for. Remember to count your blessings. Focus on the good in your life."

The nurse left and Emily sat up. Weakly, she reached an arm over into her bag and took out a card she had saved. It was a card with a beautiful angel, arms open, on the front.

Happy Birthday, My Beautiful Goldietop.
    Sweetheart, don't think for a moment that because you can't see me or hear me, I'm not thinking of you. You are in my

heart every second. I love you and hold you close. Happy 17th birthday.

All my love, Your Len

She held it close to her chest and rose to fix her hair and dress for her visitors. Waiting on the rooftop veranda, she heard her fourteen-year-old sister's voice, chipper. Emily rose and started walking, but her parents, Clara, and Len rushed toward her before she had gone two steps. They held and kissed her all at once. Emily's mother stepped back and scooped up Emily's face, examining her.

"My baby, I wish I could fix this," she said. "I wish God would just take this hurt away." She heaved a heavyhearted sigh and held Emily in her arms tightly, rocking.

"I'm okay, Mum," Emily said, but her voice betrayed her.

"Come," the woman said to Clara. "Let's give her a minute to talk with her beau. It will cheer her."

Clara pecked her sister's cheek and walked to the edge of the veranda with her mother. They looked out at the wilderness of the state forest, breathing in the mountain air that was thought to be a cure, while Len sat next to his girlfriend.

"Sweetheart, I haven't heard much from you." He put a hand on top of her hands, folded in her lap.

"I'm so sorry, Len." She looked into his eyes and held his gaze. *How handsome. He's still my dream guy in every way. If only.*

"You're so quiet this time," Len said.

"My friend, Frankie—I wrote to you about her in my letters—"

"The one that reminds you of Red? Yeah, I remember. She taught you how to jitterbug."

"Yes. Well, she had a treatment." Emily started to cry and then calmed herself. "My friend, Len—she came out dead."

"What?"

"She was one of the ones. This treatment. They hit the wrong spot, a vein with the needle, and that's it. They come out, head covered up, and that's it. She's gone."

Wrapping an arm around her shoulder, Len pulled her close.

"I'm sorry," he said.

"Len, everything has changed. I don't know how to keep on like this," she rested her head on his broad shoulder.

"No, not everything," he said.

"Yes, it has. I was a girl when I came. Now I know death and dying. I've seen it over and over. I always tried to learn from everything, but I can't make sense of this. Home isn't the same. Mary Agnes is married. Baby Clara is a teenager and taller than me now. This war—the whole world is shifting and shattering. I don't know how to hold on. I can't be the same either."

Len looked directly into her eyes.

"Listen, Honey. Listen to me. There's something that hasn't changed. It's you and me. I knew when I met you that we are going to be together. I know it now, just the same. I'm the same."

"But I'm not," she said.

"Yes, you are. I didn't fall in love with you just because you were a sweet girl. I didn't love you because you were healthy. I loved you because you are Emily Lesso, my dream girl. It's something about you I can't explain. I'm in love with who you are, your heart. That won't ever change.

"Listen, I have to tell you something. That night we met at the basketball game. Think of it. Remember it?"

Emily nodded and smiled.

"I was supposed to leave that next morning."

"What do you mean, leave?"

"I was supposed to go to CC camp, the Conservation Corps, the next day in New Mexico. They were going to build a dam and they needed strong boys. I enlisted. I was going to get paid twenty-one dollars a month to help out my parents. I was signed up for six months, me and my one buddy, Hobbs. You know I've been working since I was sixteen after my dad had a heart attack. Well, I've been working long before that, but that's when they pulled me out of school to work full time for the family. Well, I was signed up for this camp the night we met. The night I met you, I was out with the boys for the last time. My bags were packed. I was going to leave. Then I met you.

"I told Pop about you. He said, 'Of *all* those pretty Italian girls—the girl from our next-door-neighbor's family, *all* those girls at our church after you—you pick her? Why would you pick a skinny little Slovak girl?' I told him I couldn't explain it, but there was something about you.

"I told Mum I was going to stay, that I had to stay. I called the CC camp the next day and told them. I wasn't going to lose you. I had a reason to stay. I don't know how I knew, but I just knew.

"You've got a reason to stay, too."

"You are amazing, Lenny. I didn't know about CC camp," Emily said, and her head dropped. "But I don't even know how to keep on anymore. I don't know why you should wait for me."

Len held her with both arms to his chest.

"Honey, you will keep on. I know you will. Remember when they first sent you here? Remember what you said? You said, 'I'll be fine, and at least I don't have to take tests at school anymore.'" Len chuckled.

"No matter what it is, you just find the good. You were always upbeat, Honey. This just doesn't make sense, but it doesn't have to. You have to keep on, have to know there's something for you and me. Why else would we have met at the game—two people in all this big world? God brought us together, Honey.

"Just stop thinking. Just dance with me."

Wiping away tears, Emily stood. April sun peeked through clouds as they made slow circles in the middle of the veranda. With a smile of approval, Emily's mother watched from the ledge. Head tilted, Clara lifted her hand to her heart. Len hummed Bing Crosby's "Who Wouldn't Love You?" in Emily's ear, her head on his shoulder.

God, please, please, this is too much for me. Let us be together. Let me live. What did you create me for? What's my reason?

It was Len who answered. "We were made to be together, Honey. See?" She stopped swaying, dizzy, and held on to him.

———

The nurse called her name. Visiting hours were over.

Her family and her beau left so that she could go to dinner. The new doctor had insisted that Emily not miss another meal. After seeing her struggle, Nurse Nancy had convinced the doctors to let a few of the girls join Emily for dinner in her building. It would help Emily eat; perk up, she'd said. The girls spent their afternoon sunning session on the veranda, watching Emily with her handsome visitor with awe. Along the table, Emily saw the girls' faces, filled with love and trying to hope, looking at her.

"That was pretty dancing," Edith said. "How does he know how to dance so good?"

Emily put down her fork and told Edith and Rose the story.

"Well, it was his sister, Cynthia. She taught him to dance before he came to my prom. They practiced and practiced. All his buddies watched from the window at prom while the orchestra played. They couldn't believe he could dance either."

Emily remembered swaying to Tommy Dorsey's "Sinner Kissed an Angel" and Len holding her, back when things seemed simpler.

She made it through a few bites of chicken. All of her insides, her soul, her world, it was all falling in. She stood and ran to her room. One of the nurses—Emily hadn't learned her name yet—moved to stop her, but Nancy blocked the bigger woman and pleaded.

The room full of beds was empty. Late afternoon sun streamed through, but Emily shut every curtain furiously and kicked at a bin of spit cups. She threw herself on her bed, sobbing.

I've never questioned you before. I've never said this isn't fair, but I'm so far gone. Please, please, God, let me live. Why did you bring Len and I together if I can't be with him? I can't do this alone anymore. Please, please be with me. If you'll just let me live, I promise. I promise, I'll spend the rest of my life giving.

I'll never miss church. I'll do whatever you guide me to do. You've shown me purpose, but why let me die here? I want to do your purpose, your plan, and I'll do it with love. Let me live, and I'll do it. I want it. Won't you save me? Save me from this, be with me. I'll devote the rest of my life to you. Let me live. Let me live for Len. Please, let me live. I want to live, God.

Head clenched in her hands, she begged over and over. She slept, in a heap of tears and agony, on her bed.

CHAPTER 8

When the 7 a.m. bell sounded the next morning, Emily was praying again, this time without desperation. Nothing looked the same to her. The sanatorium walls, the table for breakfast—it all was temporary. She was being readied for something worthwhile.

"Are you okay today, Emily?" It was one of her new roommates, toast in hand, at breakfast.

"Yes, I am." Emily flashed a warm, glowing smile. She wrote to Len after her morning meal.

> My Lenny,
>
> I don't know how to describe this. You don't know what you've given me. You are right; I know we are meant to be together. Thank you, Love, for being strong and helping me be strong again.
>
> I asked God. I begged him to let me live. I don't know how it will happen, but I know it will. I'm certain. I know we'll be together. When you left, I poured out my heart to him. I can't even explain what happened, but I know when I woke up, someone was holding me, my entire body, in his arms. I know it was Jesus, Honey. I know it. He held on to me. He carried me. He's still with me. He promised me a life full of love. I'm not alone anymore. I pray, and someone is listening. He's told

me I'll live and I will. I don't know when, but I'm going to
make it home, and we will be together.

                                    Thank you for your love, Emily

"Emily, I'm so glad to see this change," Nancy said. "You don't know what
a gift you have."

Stifling a cough, Emily hugged Nancy.

"Your words meant so much," Emily said. "I hope I can lift up others the
way you have lifted me."

"You do, Emily. You do it without trying."

That night, Emily got approval to walk back to the Preventatorium to be
with the girls, gathered round the radio on the floor.

"Remember the night we danced?" Rose's face lit.

"I do, Rose. Frankie gave us a sweet gift, didn't she? We all have a gift, a reason."

Rose put her head in Emily's lap, and Emily combed the girl's ash-blond
hair with her fingers.

"Let's do it again for her," Emily said. "I'd guess she's watching."

"Like an angel," Edith agreed.

Nurse Margaret looked on as the girls spun, smiling, on the game room
floor. Even Irene set her book down to join. Margaret tuned the radio station,
looking for music. Instead, she stopped on a news broadcast. It was about the
war. Though administrators took steps to shield the girls from talk of the World
War (they certainly had their own battle for health to wage in the sanatorium
walls), it was impossible to hide everything. This time, Nurse Margaret, whose
own son just was drafted, couldn't help stopping the radio dial.

A newscaster spoke of North Africa. Intelligence analysts, he said,
indicated that Italy's fascist leaders likely were preparing to invade Libya.
There was no way to tell just how far they planned to go. Much of North
Africa was colonized. The Allies were preparing to fend them off. No word
at this point whether the United States would send troops.

Margaret shut the program off abruptly and turned to the girls.

"Okay. It's off to bed."

CHAPTER 9

A nervous-looking Nurse Abigail led Emily to the treatment room, but dread had lost its grip. *I carry peace in the midst of chaos*, she thought. *God is bigger than my circumstances.*

This time, happily, she noticed there was no large needle on a rolling tray, but her new doctor, Dr. Scalp, looked angry. Helping Emily off the scale, Abigail named the number, "Ninety pounds."

The doctor didn't scribble in a notebook. He kept his back to them and reviewed a long row of X-ray films.

"This damn disease," he muttered. "Just have her sit down. Ms. Heiple, I have news."

"I'm Emily Lesso."

"Yes, yes, you are. I'm sorry." He combed fingers through his gray hair. "I've been through the ringer already today, trying to figure out who can survive this change and who can't live through this, this turn for the worst. It seems we get no relief here."

Dr. Scalp was silent, staring at X-ray films of Emily's lungs. Abigail helped Emily undress to her slip and sit on the end of the hospital bed.

"Let's have a listen," Dr. Scalp said, and he held his stethoscope to her back in four places, asking her to breathe as deeply as she could manage. He kept his face positioned as far from her as he could, straining uncomfortably.

"Goddamn it," he said. "She needs it. She needs it today. She needs it right now. Tell me, Abigail, what am I to do? What the hell am I supposed to do?"

Abigail squirmed, and Dr. Scalp paced and looked at the films again.

Turning, he looking at Emily's eyes for the first time ever. "Ms. Lesso, Emily, you're what, seventeen?"

"Yes, sir."

"You've been here more than a year, correct?"

"Yes, sir, closer to two."

He sighed, sat, and let his shoulders slump. Taking off his glasses, he rubbed his eyes.

"This is bad news," he said, slipping the eyeglasses back on and regaining composure.

"You'd think a break would come, some better treatment. After all these years of study, the gas is the best we can do for you, for any of the girls in poor shape. You need a treatment. You need it immediately. Your lungs are entirely spent, and the infection has grown. It's still growing. You'll die without the treatment, no question."

After a long pause, he said it: "The equipment is broken. Our machines are broken, and we've no way to repair them for at least two weeks."

"What do you mean?" The ideas couldn't connect. His message made no sense.

"This damned war. All our machinists, all of our metal and our smarts—this battle for health has all but been forgotten. I can't get the equipment repaired because the facilities, the manufacturers, all have been converted. They're making war equipment. They're fighting for the cause. I guess we all are, even without trying, even when it's to our patients' great detriment."

"So it will be weeks before I'll have another treatment?"

"Ms. Lesso, Miss Emily, I'm so sorry to say this. It will be weeks until our machines can get to the only manufacturer still working on these."

"So I'll have to wait for treatment."

The doctor shook his head violently.

"You can't wait."

He turned swiftly, stood over the counter where her X-rays were lined up, and pushed them all off the countertop in one furious sweep of his left hand.

"I can't help you at all. But it won't be the first time I've failed, will it? And I'll fail again. We're nothing against this old plague."

Defiant, Emily shook.

"No, no, this isn't right," she said. "This isn't right. See, I have a reason. I have life before me. God has told me so."

The doctor looked back at her, blank-faced.

"It's not about what you can do or what you can't do. I have a life before me, a purpose, and you can't change it. Tuberculosis can't take it away. No one can rob me of it. See, I have a beau." She started into her story, but Dr. Scalp stopped her, gruff now, suddenly impatient.

"Then you had better write a good-bye letter."

"How can you say that?"

"It's my duty to be honest to you. Your bravery, though, it's inspiring." Bitterness and sarcasm rang out in his tone.

In turmoil, Emily spoke. "This is not right. This is not the way. I know Jesus was there. I know what he meant. I'm not to go like this."

"Well, it's good he was there, because I'm not in the business of performing miracles."

Thick silence settled for agonizing minutes.

"We'll have to phone your mother. Abigail, look up the telephone number, please."

Emily tried to reason with the doctor while the nurse was away. He did not respond.

He grabbed a slip of paper and reached for the rotary dial on the phone at his desk in a corner.

"I need Mary Lesso. I need her immediately. Right now. Yes, there's something wrong. Yes, it is an emergency. It's about her daughter. Please hurry."

Abigail wrapped an arm around the girl, trembling now on the hospital bed.

"Is this Mary Lesso? This is the sanatorium.

"No, it's not good. No, she's not. She's unwell and getting worse.

"I know you were just here. Something has changed. She's still getting worse, and we are unable to continue treatment.

"Because the war, that's why." The doctor banged his fist on his desk.

"Our machines are shut down for weeks at least. She's one of the ones who simply cannot go without it. She can't live without it.

"No, she's not okay. She can't wait for treatment, and I have no other facility with an opening.

"She's going to die.

"Yes, I am certain."

From across the treatment room, Emily could hear her mother's frantic tone but couldn't make out the words, either because she was too far away or because Emily's own thoughts were swirling wildly. *This does not fit. It doesn't make sense.*

"I strongly recommend you do not, absolutely not. Believe me, the end of TB is the worst a person can endure. You don't want her to die that way, without professional help."

This time, Emily heard her mother's shouting clearly.

"If she is going to die, it will be in her own home, with her family. I will be there tomorrow. I'm coming to get my baby."

"Do whatever you want. If you want her to die without comfort, that's your decision, not mine."

The doctor slammed down the receiver.

CHAPTER 10

Packing her things, Emily froze.

That photo of Len and her picnicking outside—it was young love, pure and uncomplicated.

"I don't understand. I don't understand. I don't understand." Emily whispered the words over and over.

"You don't have to. Just trust." It was a nurse standing behind her, someone Emily didn't recognize. Her long, white hair lay on her shoulders, without the net many of the nurses wore. "Let me see this."

Surprised, Emily showed the photograph to the older woman. She and Len were happy, smiling on a handmade rug spread across grass. It was a sunny day kind of memory, and nothing could make it fade. The nurse squinted and held the photo at arm's length.

"Wow. He's dreamy," she said. "You make a handsome couple, and I bet you'll have beautiful babies, too. Never you mind Dr. Scalp. He's under strain like never before. You keep holding to what you already know." The nurse gave the treasure back to Emily, who tucked it lovingly in an envelope and slipped it into a Bible sitting at the bottom of her bag.

"You talked to the doctor about me? I haven't seen you here before. You're new?"

There was no answer. The woman was gone. Only one other woman in her ward, Mary, was resting nearby.

"Who's the new nurse?" Emily asked.

Confused, Mary just looked at her with tired eyes.

"I'm sorry, Em. I was resting. I don't know what you mean. Who?"

"Never mind, Mary." Emily smiled, prayed thanks, and finished packing.

Emily hardly could sleep that night. In the darkness, she saw shapes of the women next to her, all breathing deeply, some wheezing.

How many nights have I been here, in a sanatorium bed? Can it be true that I'll be at home tomorrow?

Excitement rose in her chest until coughing took over. Over and over the cough shook her body until she spat dark crimson onto a kerchief. That's why she was going back. That's what the doctor had said: She was to die. But she wouldn't go like the others. She'd have her good-byes. She'd be home again, tucked safe in her own bed, in the house that smelled some of boiled cabbage but more like candle wax, prayers burning and rising up in wisps to Mary. She could speak to Len, tell him what she'd known and what God had said. Maybe it was in heaven where they'd be together. That was okay. That was a fate she could welcome. But it didn't seem to be what the angel was saying: *Keep holding to what you already know.*

Mary's heavy wheezing brought her focus to her friends, the suffering around her.

I'll never see the girls in the Preventatorium again.

Emily spent the rest of the night praying for the girls—Pauline, Rose, Edith, Bernice, so many others. It was the early hours of morning before slumber took her.

The next morning was the first time she overslept the bell.

"Hurry, Emily. Let's get you bathed. You've a lot of exit paperwork to sign." It was Heidi tugging on Emily's right arm. Heidi rushed the girl through breakfast and agreed to escort her again to the Preventatorium for good-byes afterward.

In the hall, the girls gathered round their loving friend.

"I can't believe you're leaving, Emily," Pauline said. "Who will we dance with now?"

"You can always dance. Dancing and praying, you don't have to be anywhere special or even with anyone special. No matter how far from home—" Emily stopped. "Don't ever give up on hoping or dancing or praying, girls." She wasn't speaking directly to any of the girls at that moment. "Have faith no matter what anyone says. I'll be thinking of you all and holding you in my heart."

"Well, I wish you were going to be here to hold us in person." Edith wrapped her arms around Emily's legs and started crying.

"Okay, let's not get into hysterics," Heidi scolded. "Remember what happened last time you were all worked up, Edith?"

Fighting against Heidi's grip, Emily kneeled down to Edith and Rose next to her.

"You're both princesses, remember that. Someone loves you princesses dearly," Emily turned to Pauline. "Take over the beauty parlor for me, please. These girls need someone to fix their hair."

"That is enough. Let's get you back to the main building and the nurse's station for papers, now." Heidi ushered Emily briskly downstairs to a waiting van that drove them to the central building.

"Sit down. First is a release of information so we can send our records to your doctor, if you see him."

The stack of papers was half an inch thick.

Emily started to flip through the pages.

"Hurry now. We don't have time to meander. Next is a paper confirming you've returned all sanatorium belongings and then is a release of liability, that this decision to leave our care is your own choice and we can't be held responsible for whatever may happen."

Emily was reluctant to pick up a pen.

"I told you to hurry." Heidi's voice was getting frantic.

"But why? My mother doesn't arrive for another hour, and I've nothing else to do. You won't even let me say a proper good-bye."

"Don't get smart, miss," Heidi said. "Just sign."

Irritated, Emily signed the first few slips of paper. Her eyes settled on a document titled "Agreement for Necessary Surgery." She looked up at Heidi.

"Don't worry. That's only if you're healthy enough for surgery. I'm sorry to put it so plainly, but I think we both know that's unlikely."

"But wait. What surgery?"

"Don't question. Just sign."

Squinting, Emily read through the tiny words, finally reaching the description of surgery: *tubal ligation*. She threw down the pen and stood.

"I'm finished here. I won't sign anything further."

"Oh, really," Heidi put her hands on her hips. "You will sign, and you'll do so now, this moment."

Emily didn't move.

"I told you, Emily. It is required."

"By who?"

"The authorities!" Heidi was screaming now, red-faced, arms in the air.

Emily sat, threw the stack of papers in the trash and crossed her arms firmly.

"Who knows what else you wanted me to sign?"

"This is for your good, Emily, and not just yours. If you did somehow survive without treatment and then one day became pregnant, you would die and so would the fetus."

The girl didn't budge.

"And say, for sake of argument only, you and the infant both miraculously lived. How could you ever care for a child? Look at your state. Let me remind you there is no known cure. You'll be an invalid for whatever time is left for you. You trying to take care of a child? Imagine that. Just imagine it. It would be a curse for both of you."

Emily shut out the cruel words.

"That's fine. You're not leaving until you sign. You can sit there as long as you want. I don't care. I'm through trying to help you."

With relief, Emily saw her mother, dressed in a brown hat and skirt suit, clicking up the steps in thick-heeled shoes. She was early.

"My Emilia." She held her child. "It's finally time to come home."

"Thank goodness you're here, Mrs. Lesso." Heidi softened her tone. "We were having trouble with your daughter. She refuses to cooperate."

"What's this?"

"Mum, they want me to say I'll never have children. They want me to agree to surgery for it."

"Well, nurse, what on earth does that have to do with what we're here for today? Does she really need to be harangued about this?"

Heidi, disgusted, threw up her hands.

"Well, I guess now we know where she gets it. Forget you both. I'm trying to help, but you won't listen. I'll get the doctor."

"Mum, don't let them do it." Emily held close to her mother.

"Of course not. How ridiculous. I knew this place was a disaster. I'm so thankful you'll be home. Nurse, I will speak to the doctor privately."

"I'll bring him out to talk sense to both of you."

"No. I will speak to him without you. Thank you. If you won't show me, I'll find him myself."

Short, fierce, Emily's mother stomped down the hallway, hat brim bouncing up and down with each clack of her shoes. Opening every door until she came to the last, the cramped, white-walled treatment room, she slammed the door behind her.

It swung back open a few minutes later. Mrs. Lesso emerged, smashed her hat down on her head in triumph, and marched toward her daughter.

"Let me get your bags. The neighbor was very kind to drive us without notice. We'll not keep him waiting."

"We're through here."

She took her daughter's arm in one hand and a sack of clothes in the other and guided her down the stairs and out the grand entryway. Summer's greenery surrounded them. Mr. Hrushevksy stepped out and opened the trunk for Emily's sack. He helped Mrs. Lesso and Emily into the car and drove them down past the Preventatorium. Emily rolled down her window.

Six or seven girls were crowded onto one balcony, waving and smiling.

There was Nurse Nancy in the middle, shorter than the teenage girls. Irene was there, too, and Bernice. Emily turned to keep waving as the vehicle pulled away, still waving when the road and the trees overhead and on every side were all she could see.

"What did the doctor say to you, Mum?"

"Absolute nonsense."

"How did you get him to say I could go without signing?"

Emily's mother patted the girl's hand.

"He didn't."

CHAPTER 11

JUNE 1942 Len watched as his mother packed two lunches—slices of salami, Italian bread, and peaches—in a brown sack. Morning sun beamed in through yellow gingham curtains in the kitchen near the counter where she worked. Rising pasta dough was pushing up an old dish towel in a bowl beside her. She handed Len and his father the bags and stepped on the back porch with them. To her son, she gave a peck on the cheek and to her husband, a squeeze and a firm kiss on the lips. "Love you, Yoil," she said, using the pet name they made for each other.

The two men stepped down into the yard.

"Love you, Len." She was waving already, even though they were just a few steps away on a dirt path through the backyard garden.

The almost eighteen-year-old turned back with a look of admiration and pride, too. He was helping to care for the family. "Love you, Mum."

He walked slowly next to his father through rows of tomato, sprouting green and fragrant and clinging with ropey fingers on poles, and then low-lying zucchini spreading leaves on the ground. A few dandelion plants stretched here and there.

"Could use weeding," Len's father remarked.

"Maybe tonight, Pop."

When they reached the back gate, they both turned one last time. There was Len's mother on the porch, sweeping leaves, wearing a white apron over her skirt. She tucked the broom under an arm and blew quick kisses in the air. Len heard the screen door shut behind her as they clicked the wooden gate. They could already see the mill and other men lining up to punch in, lunch buckets in hand. The front office for the Standard Tin Plate Company swarmed with men, many of them Len's neighbors, but no others his age. Boys his age were finishing high school or working their first jobs at less physically demanding posts—mixing shakes at the local soda joint, delivering the newspaper, or taking tickets at the movie house. This place was for hardworking men who were providing for their families.

"Son, I wish we had ten like you." It was Len's direct supervisor, the superintendent, a portly fellow nicknamed Smitty. "I looked over your reports yesterday afternoon. You're keeping a close eye on every detail. We need that. And the men seem to like you, even though you're probably young enough to be a son to any one of them. It's hard to believe you started just this year. I'm not sure we've ever promoted a lineman to foreman in such a short period, and I know we've never had a foreman so young."

"Thank you, sir. My family really could use this money."

"Well, we're glad to have you, though I do wonder if a fellow like you should be out pursuing other things." Smitty sat behind a big metal desk and twisted the edges of his handlebar mustache. "Did you finish school?"

"No."

"How old were you when you left?"

"Sixteen."

"Now why? You're bright. Didn't you do well? Maybe a good-looking boy like you was distracted with other things." The older man tipped his head, pulled a Lucky Strike from a drawer, and lit it. Smoke spread around the small office space, hot already and it wasn't even 8 a.m.

"Come on, now. I've seen the way the ladies in the can factory get when you're around," his boss pressed.

Len fidgeted. He started to answer.

"It's nothing like that."

"Oh, you're still seeing that Slovak girl?"

"Yes, sir," Len nodded.

"That's right. Your dad was telling me that when I was over for spaghetti. She's away, sick, isn't she? Aren't you afraid you'll get her disease? You know the foreman before you had to leave because he had it. I'd hate to see that for you, too. I don't want any of that around here."

Len shook his head.

"Well, never mind all that, I guess. I'm just happy you're here. I won't keep you from your work. I need you to look over mills 10 to 15 closely today. We need to make sure we're up to quota. I'm expecting another big order later this week. We need to be, or keep, working like a well-oiled machine here." Smitty drew on his cigarette long and slow. "Now that we're roped into this war, Uncle Sam's going to need every factory ready to produce."

"Do you think—?" Len started.

"It doesn't matter what I think. We need to be prepared."

"Yes, sir. Thank you." Len was glad to get out of the cramped, smoke-filled room. He knew now how to tell when the boss was done talking. He thought of the day his life had changed from boyhood to manhood. He was just sixteen when the principal had called for him.

He had a big wrestling match coming up. Rather than skipping meals and water to make a lower weight, like the other boys at Canonsburg High, Len had been focused on beating anyone he was set up against. He didn't shy away from wrestling anybody—didn't matter if he was bigger. Len was better and he knew it. He and his buddy were in the gym, practicing. He had him in a pinch head lock on the mat when one of his teachers called out his name.

"What's that?" Len looked up, and his friend wriggled free.

"Mr. Bradley wants to see you," he said.

"Oh, boy, Len. What'd you do now?" His liberated buddy was grinning.

"Nothing. I don't think," he said, with a wink. Len stood and walked toward the teacher. "What's the matter?"

"I have no idea. I just know the principal needs you in his office."

"But what did I do?"

"I don't know. Nothing. Just go see him."

Len's friend snickered. "Somebody's in trouble."

"You shush your mouth." Len strutted over to the locker room and dressed quickly.

The principal kept his face down, reading a note through thick glasses, when Len walked into his office. The boy sat, and Mr. Bradley did, too, behind his desk. Folding his glasses and setting them aside, he reached for something beneath a pile of paperwork and then slid a paper toward Len.

"Sign your name there."

"What for?"

"Working papers."

"What do you mean? I don't have a job. I'm in school."

"Well, as of today, that's changed. You've got to go find a job now that your dad's in the hospital with a heart attack. If you want your mother to keep putting food on the table, you better go look for a job, a real job. Your school days are over, son."

And there was his dad, almost two years after the heart attack hit, bent over his work along the line at the mill, sweat matting dark hair on his forehead. He struggled, tongs in hand, bending and warping sheets of tin stuck together. Len resisted the urge to go talk to him, check on him. He'd been scolded enough for that. His dad didn't want anyone thinking his boy, now their boss, favored him. Maybe there was something he could do for him, something no one would see.

Len walked over to where men in work aprons, faces shielded with masks, pulled out pieces of glowing metal with long-handled tongs. He sensed the oven's heat and felt burning metallic air, thick, coat his throat with every breath. It was part of his duties to tell the men which sheets to send down which lines. The thinner ones would be easier to handle and pull apart, and better yet if they were smooth, without the lumps that would make the tin alloy tough to separate. He glanced back at his father farther down the line.

His face was red, cheeks trembling with exertion. Waving one of the men close to him, Len leaned toward his ear. The clang of tools made it impossible to get anything across without shouting.

"Send these four down this line," Len yelled, pointing to a stack of ones he knew were more pliable. "And these two here."

The man shook his head.

Len yelled the instructions louder, and the worker shook his head and gave an okay signal with a gloved hand.

"And keep it like that, will ya? The ones that come out like that, just send them down line No. 3."

The man gave another quick nod and turned back toward the open oven.

Long days at the mill had made Len restless. He'd always worked and worked hard, but all this talk of war made something stir inside him. He wanted to be fighting. He was a fighter. It just had to be put to good use.

Reading his mind, one of the linemen asked Len whether the big boss had said anything about the mill being converted to a plant for army equipment. Feeling he had to keep conversations with the superintendent to himself, Len shrugged.

"I really don't know what's going to happen," he said. "Doesn't seem like anybody does."

"Well, that's the truth, isn't it?" The lineman went back to his tinkering but turned back. "You're about drafting age, right? You could be gone any day now, Lenny."

"I suppose. That's if I pass the physical."

The worker chuckled.

"Strong young man like you, used to workin' hard. You're just the type they need."

The words lifted Len's heart. He was no dodger, and he wasn't afraid.

A few more rounds at the other mills and it was a few minutes past lunch time. Len wasn't one to leave a job unfinished while he took a break. At the main office, he looked for his father. They usually ate together outside, but there was no sign of his dad. He'd likely already eaten, but his absence gave Len an uneasy feeling. *Thank goodness I was able to get him a break, though. This job is good for something.* Len sat alone under the shade of a maple tree and opened his sack lunch. A few other men were eating from metal boxes at a picnic table nearby.

Len looked at his home and smiled. *What a childhood I've had. Everyone on my street was my buddy. We all made our own fun, together. We all worked together and got along. When it was time to prepare a garden, we'd get out the tools and do everybody's house. When a day of hard work was over, Pop pulled out his old accordion. We'd dance a tarantella right out in the street. Maybe I'll ask him to pull it out tonight and a jug of his homemade wine, too.*

When it was time to clock out that day, his dad was silent. He wouldn't look at Len.

"What is it, Pop? Are you okay?" Len asked as they walked up a hill toward their back gate. A gentle rain was falling, and the skies had turned gray. The man, red-faced, scowled at his son and strode ahead of him. At home, he slammed the kitchen door. Len followed in behind, but his dad didn't speak until he'd washed the grease from his hands and wiped his face on a hand towel.

"Son, don't you do that no more to me, not ever."

Len's mom walked to the kitchen but kept back in a corner when she heard her husband's tone.

"What, Pop?"

"You know what. I know what you did. Everybody knows it," he said. "I worked there for thirty years. Those guys are my buddies."

"I was just trying to help you," Len said. "Dad, I can't just watch you pull your guts out. I can't watch it. You're my dad. I love you."

His dad huffed. "You don't do that to them, Len. Maybe there you're the boss, but at home, I'm the boss. That's all I'll say."

Wounded, Len pulled his earnings from his pocket and laid them on the table: $8.05. His dad softened.

"Thank you, son."

Len walked to his mother and gave her a kiss on the cheek. She patted his face.

"My Lenny, Nadaduch," she whispered. "Thank you."

By sunset, Len had eaten, written to his Goldietop, Emily, and weeded the backyard at his place and at the neighbor's. Maybe his dad would see that the dandelions were gone when they went together to the mill the next day.

CHAPTER 12

Finally home, Emily walked up the front steps and over the same creaky planks on the porch. She paused at the open doorway. The familiar sight was what she'd imagined and longed for, but she didn't know it would feel like this. *How could everything be the same and yet so different all at once?*

"Let's go on in now, Emilia," her mother said.

The neighbor who drove them home moved past them and set Emily's bag on the floor.

"My Emilia! Oh, is my baby home?" Emily's father ran to greet her. He scooped her up.

"How I've missed you," he said, spinning her around. "I knew you'd be all right."

Tears streamed down Emily's face as her father held her tightly.

"Thank you, Pop, for coming to visit me and for what you said."

He kissed her forehead.

"What do you mean?" He kissed her head once more.

"You always told me, 'You'll be all right.'" Emily smiled at her father.

"Of course, Emilia," he said, switching to Slovak. "You're thin now, but I know you'll be all right. This is how children are made strong."

"Pop, I still need those words. Thank you. I love you." Emily pressed her cheek to his chest.

"I love you, too, Emilia," he said. "You are home now and your mother will fatten you up and have you running around again soon, like it never happened. No worries. Let's get you to bed for rest." He picked up her bag, and Emily and her mother followed him up the stairwell that led to her bedroom. Setting the bag down outside her door, he hugged her once more.

"Sleep, Emilia," he said, giving her a kiss on the cheek. "Get better now."

Memories flooded over her as Emily opened the door to the room that overlooked the backyard. Her bed was in a corner opposite the door with the same white crochet blanket from her grandmother that kept her warm in winter. She could picture the three sisters sitting on the edge of that bed chatting, singing familiar tunes, and taking turns brushing each other's hair and rolling it in rags for church the next morning.

Her mother helped her change into her pajamas.

"I don't know that I'm tired yet, Mum," she said.

"You need rest, Emilia." Her mother ushered her to bed and covered her with a light blanket. "Don't worry about anything. Just rest. Clara will be home this afternoon to see you."

As soon as she laid her head on the pillow, Emily felt a wave of exhaustion. The long ride from the sanatorium had taken its toll, and she could feel it now. It was all she could to do keep her eyes open as her mother kissed her and pulled the blanket up near her shoulders. Floating in the haze between awake and asleep, she heard her mother and father talking outside her room.

"Well, what are they saying now?" Her father's voice was deep and full of concern, a tone he'd hidden when he was speaking to Emily.

"Well, Emory, I don't know."

"What do you mean? They made us send her. They were supposed to be helping her. What did they even do?"

"Well, a lot of those treatments."

"Well, if she's not better, why is she home?"

"Because there's nothing else to do now that the equipment is down." Emily heard her mother's voice crack with grief.

"I don't know how that can be. There has to be something else they can do."

Emily heard sobbing stifled quickly and then the door cracked open. She tried with all her might to raise her eyelids but didn't have the strength. She tried to reach out to her mother with her hand but couldn't lift it. She couldn't move any part of her body to gesture. She heard her mother drop at the edge of her bed and pray. "Our Father, who art in Heaven. Hallowed be thy name. Thy Kingdom come. Thy will be done, on earth as it is in Heaven. Heal this child, please. Will you hear our prayers? Heal our daughter."

With every bit of strength she had left, Emily prayed silently along with her mother until she succumbed to sleep.

It was mid-afternoon when Clara burst through the front door.

"Is Emily back?"

Their mother looked up from scrubbing the kitchen floor.

"She's asleep, but yes, she is finally home."

"Oh, can I please see her?" Clara was halfway up the stairs already. "I can't wait a minute longer, Mum, and I've brought someone Emily will be happy to see," Clara said. Waiting at the doorway was Red, Emily's schoolgirl friend, the one who looked a bit like Frankie.

"All right, girls, but just for a minute." The older woman smiled at the girls. The house was full of girls again. The two hurried to the bedroom at the top of the steps and opened the door slowly.

"Em," Clara whispered, shaking her sister's shoulder. "Oh, sis, you're home."

After a moment, Emily yawned, squinting, and sat up.

"Clara, it's you. I've missed you," she said.

"You, too, sis," Clara said. "I love you."

Emily tried to answer but a cough scratched in the back of her throat. Trying to stymie it before it grew into a coughing spell, she curled away from her sister and coughed into her elbow.

"I'll go and get you water," Clara said.

Still coughing, Emily nodded. Her head throbbed. She felt sweat slide down one side of her brow and wiped it away.

"Oh, I've brought someone to see you, too."

Red stood near the door, hair curled and wearing a dress Emily recognized. She had helped her make it. Red smiled but didn't move any closer.

"Emily, I'm so sorry," she said.

The cough had finally stopped and Emily tried to clear her throat to speak. Her voice was scratchy and hardly audible.

"Red, it's so good to see you. I think about you all the time."

"I think about you, too, and what fun we all used to have. It's such a pity that this happened to you. I'll never understand it, why it happened to the gentlest, sweetest one."

"Pity? I don't know," Emily answered. One more cough escaped.

"What was it like there? What did they do?"

"They did a lot of treatments."

"Like what?" Red's eyes were wide with curiosity.

"Well, first they did one with a needle in my back. It didn't seem to help, so they switched to trying it into my stomach, too."

"Weren't you afraid?"

After a moment of silence, Emily responded. "A lot of girls died that way, with the needle. If they hit a vein, you'd die in sixty seconds."

Frankie gasped and put a gloved hand over her mouth.

"So did it cure you?"

"Well, after a year, they finally got my temperature down from 103."

"How did you manage? I feel so bad you were there, locked away."

"I prayed a lot," Emily said. "It got me through."

"But you're better now?"

"Well, not yet."

"Oh, Em. I'm so sorry, but my mother would kill me if she knew I came. She told me I couldn't come because what you have can spread to anyone."

Emily just looked at the girl who used to skip with her around town, arm in arm, to church and to school.

"I told Mum that it wasn't like that, that you got this sickness from the cold.

Remember, we all thought it was from the time you walked nine miles with us in that freezing rain to celebrate our football win in the victory march?"

"Yes, Mum said I'd catch my death of cold," Emily said. "I thought that was just a saying. I should have believed her, but I was determined to go with the rest of our school."

Red kept going. "We all thought it was that. You're not still contagious?"

"Well, I am. It is bacteria. That's what the doctor said."

Red's hand was still hovering over her mouth, but her eyes grew wider still. Emily saw fear in her friend's eyes.

"Are you still going with Walter?"

"Yes, I think we'll get married next year," Red answered. "That's what everybody's saying. And you're still seeing Len?"

"Oh, yes," Emily said. "He came to visit me a lot. We wrote letters."

"That's so sweet that he loves you still, even when you're like *this*."

Emily's expression drooped as the words sank in. She started to answer but the words caught in her throat.

"Oh, Em, I didn't mean it like that," Red said. "It's just that he's not afraid, that he cares about you enough to forget what you have, to not give up when you're away."

It was too late to take back the words.

"Yes," Emily said quietly.

"I didn't mean to hurt your feelings."

Shaking her head, Emily tried to answer.

"I'm all right, just hoarse," she whispered.

"Well, I should go. Mum would be furious." Red said. "I hope I see you soon, Em. We could all four go out like we used to."

Slipping out of the room, Red offered a quick, muffled farewell from beneath her hand. Clara bumped into her in the hallway.

"You're leaving already?" Clara asked with a note of surprise.

Red stepped beside her and shuffled down the stairs, head down and ignoring Mrs. Lesso's look of concern.

———

Emily's eyes were rimmed with tears when Clara walked into the bedroom, handed a glass of water to her sister, and sat on the edge of the bed.

"How are you feeling?" she asked.

"Like an outcast."

CHAPTER 13

Emily heard the familiar click of the screen door and knew she was finally alone. She scanned the front yard in sunset's glow, savoring the quiet. Under the pear tree, purple morning glories her grandmother had planted years ago bowed and swayed with each gentle breeze. The perennial flowers already were closing gently for the evening.

She shut her eyes. Emily knew, at once, that everything at home was more or less the same, but she was different. Life moved around her in the same patterns it always had and would keep moving, breathing and growing, even if she didn't.

A clap of laughter cracked the serenity.

She looked up. A couple walked down the street toward her house. The girl's flirtatious, bubbling giggle preceded them. She wore a wide skirt that bounced up and down with her steps. *I used to walk like that,* Emily thought. She squinted, trying to make out the shapes of the healthy girl and the young man beside her. His shape was thin but muscular and his hair rose inches above his head in a mound that struck Emily as familiar. He was walking straight ahead, but the girl, endlessly amused, kept wrapping her right arm around his left and leaning in to him, overcome with laughing.

They came closer and Emily recognized the handsome escort.

It was her Len.

Dropping her feet to the ground to still the swing, Emily held her breath.

Out of habit, Lenny glanced toward her house and saw nothing. But something made him look one more time. He squinted until he could see the figure of a young woman. He was so startled to see his love on the front porch—empty for so long—that he nearly tripped. The girl kept giggling but stopped as Len pulled her arm off his again and walked away from her. She huffed and put her hands on her hips but didn't follow. Lenny ignored her pouting and bounded over and up the porch steps. He hugged Emily's shoulders tightly.

"When did you come home, Honey?"

Emily hesitated. "A few days ago."

"Why didn't you send someone for me?" he asked. "I just sent a letter to you at the sanatorium."

"I was just exhausted, and I thought you might be busy," Emily said, directing her gaze toward the girl with her arms crossed in the front yard.

"Oh, I was just taking Herb's sister to her mom's place. It was a favor, really, Em. You know how I feel," he said. "I told you how I feel. You are my Goldietop. There's no one else but you; there never could be. I knew it since I first saw you."

Emily relaxed her shoulders and let a smile turn up the corners of her mouth.

"Well, I can't be mad. You don't know what it meant to me when you visited me *there*," she said.

"I had to see you." He smiled and squeezed both her hands in his. "Why are you back? You were so sick last time. I think you do look better, but you're always beautiful to me. I knew it. I knew you were going to beat it, Sweetheart."

She looked down at their hands.

"It's not that. They sent me home, so I could be here when. . . ." Her voice trailed off. "They said there was nothing left to do."

The silence sank in around them. Lenny shook his head in defiance. *Those doctors don't know everything.*

"It's all right." She was trembling now. "They gave up hope, but I'm not going to do that. I can't do that. I know this isn't all there is for me. There's you. I prayed. I told God that. I begged him."

"I know this is not it, Sweetheart." Lenny sat next to her. "God doesn't work that way. We belong together."

"But, Len, what if I don't have that much time? What if what the doctors say is true?" She looked up at his face, those eyes that melted her to her core.

Lenny stood and leaned his muscular frame over her and looked into her eyes. He spoke slowly.

"I will take every minute I can get."

She smiled. She felt tears and unspoken fear and longing swell in her soul. He moved his face closer still.

"I'm serious. I mean it. I want to be with you every minute I can. Every second you're here on this earth, I want to be the man next to you, the man caring for you."

He knelt down in front of the porch swing and held her right hand to his heart.

"You mean it, Len?" Emily whispered it like a prayer.

"Yes, Emily," he said. "I love you. We're going to be a family."

Emily closed her eyes and prayed again. *Let me get better. I'll serve you. I'll go to church every day. I'll be a loving wife and mother. Thank you, God, for Len. Please, let me live for Len and our life together.*

⸺

In the months that followed, Emily wasn't sure whether her lungs were improving, but she knew her heart was. She felt confirmation of the revelation she experienced inside the sanatorium—that there was a plan for her, a beautiful life story that included Len and their children. She didn't know what she and Len would have to face to get through this, but she knew God would be her healer.

CHAPTER 14

DECEMBER 1942 In the living room, Len's older brother, Pete, was spread out on the couch, the old Davenport where he and Len slept. Now that it was winter, it was their job to keep the fire burning. They were waiting for the Jewish peddler who would be by later that day, the day before Christmas Eve, to show his wares. It was how they did their shopping and where Len's mother had bought him his favorite pair of jeans, the ones with red piping down the side.

Pete worked part-time at the can factory. It was mostly women there and older, feebler men.

"Didn't you work today?" Len asked, stretching aching shoulders and heading toward a stairwell to say hello to his sisters upstairs in their rooms.

"Nope. I worked yesterday," Pete said.

"So did I, Pete." Len started up the steps.

"Wait, Len. I need to ask you something."

"What is it now? I'm not lending you no money."

"Aw, but I wanted to take Doris out tonight. I need five dollars."

"No, Pete. You want five dollars, then why don't you work every day?" Len stopped and looked down at his older sibling, babied from birth because he was a sickly infant. He was wearing a brand-new Pandora hat Len had bought last week.

"What do you think you're doing? I just bought that. I didn't even wear it yet."

Pete, still stretched out, tipped the hat up.

"It looks good on me, though."

Len marched down the steps and grabbed it off Pete's head. With one swift motion, Pete was on his feet. He pushed his younger brother's shoulders.

"You give me that hat back," Len ordered.

"Try to take it off me, you son of a bitch."

They heard their mother gasp from the kitchen.

"Dominic!" she yelled and then stood aside as their dad rushed in to the living room with the big window that faced the street.

"Don't touch me," Len said.

Pete punched his brother's stomach and knocked him backward into the tree Len and his father had cut down together the day before. As soon as he'd recovered, Len's hands were around his brother's neck. The tree was knocked sideways.

"Don't you have respect?" Their father was furious. "Swearing and fighting, in this house, and your mother is right here. And it's almost Christmas!"

The boys kept at it, Pete grappling and throwing slaps and punches when he could, but Len had him backed against a wall.

"I said, 'Not in this house!'"

They heard their mother scream. Their father grabbed a hot poker from the fire and held it toward them. They froze. He put the glowing poker between them, and each of the boys stepped back a foot, scowling.

"That's enough now. Len, take your hat and go."

Pete slumped back onto the couch.

"Never mind him, Len." His sister, Babe, leaned against the railing, halfway down the steps. "We want to know what you've got for Emily for Christmas." Dolly, Cynthia, and Tony were lined up behind her, all in dresses.

Len had always doted on his sisters, and they returned his affection by pressing his shirts or preparing meals for him. Pete, on the other hand, mostly ignored them, except when he needed something. Reaching into his jacket pocket, Len pulled out a box with a gold chain inside with a ruby pendant. The girls let out a collective gasp, and Babe held up the necklace. The jewel glittered.

"You're really going to wow her this year. I wonder whether it's a different piece of jewelry she'll be looking for, though, Len."

The girls giggled, and Len just gave them a look.

"I know, you're waiting until after this war, and when she's feeling better." Babe gave him a squeeze. "There's no heart in town safe until you're spoken for. I'd be wanting you to propose to me, if I were Emily. We adore her, just like another sister."

"Okay, Babe, hand it back. Wait, can you help me wrap it?" Len knew his sisters could make the gift look like a treasure.

"Sure thing, Len, I'll get it looking gorgeous, though it will take her breath away as it is."

Babe and the other girls hurried up the steps to their rooms, and Len went to straighten the tree. Pete pretended to be asleep.

"No more, please, Len. It's Christmas." Len's mother put an arm on his back.

Len hugged his mom and called her honey in Italian.

"Okay, Mum, Tesoro. For you." He kissed her cheek. "Buona sera."

He shouted up to his sisters that he'd be back and barely caught the bus to Strabane for Emily's house, passing all the houses in Canonsburg stacked against each other and sparkling with Christmas lights.

When he got there, Emily was posing with her family for a photo in front of the Christmas tree. Emily was just thinking how different this scene was from last year, when the nurses in their starched white hats encouraged the girls to look "spry" in their best dresses before the sanatorium's tall tree. *Always pretending we weren't as sick as we were, until, of course, the treatment room, where our X-rays told the truth.*

Now, she was home, surrounded by her sisters and brother, Andy, who would play piano for them that night and again on Christmas Eve. They would gather there or around a Nativity scene to sing "Silent Night" and other carols in Slovak. Everyone would follow her father's rich baritone.

Emily still was sick—she had her cough to remind her—but at least she was home. The town doctor had warned her that it might be her last Christmas. He was afraid to examine her. Emily could sense it in the way he kept his head and shoulders as far away as possible, even when measuring her breathing capacity.

Her face lit at the sight of Len in the doorway through the crowded room.

"Honey!"

"Hi, Sweetheart." Len rushed through the group of friends and family, past the well-loved and worn figures in the Nativity scene, and scooped up his love in front of the tree. The house smelled of pine. When he set her down, Andy put out his hand toward Len, who hugged him instead.

"It's good to see you, Len. And it's even better to see you and Emily together. I see how happy you make her."

Andy smiled at his sister and whispered a phrase to her in Slovak.

"Pst, Andrew!" she blushed and told him to hush with a gentle tap on his arm.

"She's looking so much better, Andy, isn't she? How long are you and Helen back in town?"

"Until New Year's Eve, Len."

"Well, it's good to see you."

"Thanks, Len. Oh, come say hello to Mum. Knowing her, she's got something baking, and she's been talking about how you're helping Emily along. We all appreciate that."

Emily's mom was working over a pot of boiling water in the kitchen, and Emily rushed in before the boys to hide the scarf she'd been making for Len. She stuffed it in a drawer swiftly. Len bent down to peck both sides of the woman's face and breathed in deeply, savoring the smell of vanilla and spices.

"Len, so happy that you're here." She patted her hands on her apron, dusting away handprints of flour. "I do hope we'll see you at Mass, too?"

"Absolutely, Mum. I wouldn't miss a chance to sit with the most beautiful women in Strabane."

It was the first time Len had called her "Mum" and her eyes showed a bit of surprise. She gave a warm smile at the flattery.

"You have something to eat. We've been baking cookies all day, though they seem to be disappearing now that Andy's home. You'd better act quick."

Len smiled and sat at the table to talk to Emily's dad, Emory, who was humming Christmas carols already. Emily put her hands on her father's shoulders.

"My baby," he said. "We can have Christmas again now that you're back. It will be like it always was, you girls singing and wrapping up your old baby dolls to open again on Christmas morning, like it was the most beautiful surprise you'd ever seen."

Emily chuckled, but the laugh started up her cough and she buried her face in her elbow for a moment.

"We're older than that now, Pop. Mary Agnes is a married woman. But being together again is the best Christmas gift I can imagine."

"It is a gift to be together, and now we have this Len fellow around, too."

They all laughed, but then Mr. Lesso stopped and gave her daughter's suitor a serious look.

"You aren't going anywhere for a while, are you? What's this business about enlisting?"

"Not enlisting, Mr. Lesso. I'm drafting age. It's a service, to protect our families."

"Well, I can respect that, but I also know what it means to Emily to have you around."

Emily's mother broke in.

"No talk of war at Christmas, Emory. It's only happiness right now. That's all that's allowed." She put her hands on her hips with pretend sternness.

No one dared to disobey, and they spent a pleasant evening together and the next night, sitting together at midnight Mass, all in a row. Emily pictured a row full of her and Len's children filling a pew in that same church, looking up toward the poinsettias and the shrines, shimmering with flickering candlelight. Len squeezed her hand. *You've brought me this far, Jesus. If he must go to war, bring Len home safe and let us begin our family.* She whispered the prayer in her heart.

Underneath falling snow, he kissed her in front of her family outside St. Patrick's Cathedral, where they'd been so many times before when they were younger and Emily was healthy.

"Merry Christmas, Beautiful." He looked at her face. Curls around her glowed and shimmered in moonlight. "I'll be by tomorrow to give you your present. Okay, Sweetheart?"

He walked home in snow as deep as it was the night he'd met her at the basketball game. It seemed so long ago, but even after all her illness, her smile was as vibrant as the night he thought she was a cheerleader, the night he knew his life had changed for the better.

Before sunrise the next morning, Pete and Len put their differences aside as much as they could—meaning they ignored one another—and the family listened to Babe's smooth voice singing "Oh, Holy Night" against the crackle of the fireplace. They passed around a bowl of warm chestnuts and shared gifts—checkers and card games from the Jewish peddler—mostly trinkets because, with the war, everything was so uncertain, even if business was booming at the mill.

"Oh, Len, I hope you like the golden paper." Babe handed Len the gift she'd wrapped for him. "It was the best I have."

"She'll love it, Babe." Len gave her a kiss on the cheek.

Together on the porch swing that Christmas night, after the Lesso family had sung rounds of carols and a few Slovak melodies around the piano with Andy as their pianist, Len rocked gently, admiring the felt scarf Emily had given him.

"I got you something, too, Honey."

He handed her the small box wrapped in gold foil. Emily turned it around in her hands and smiled, opening it gently to save the paper.

"It's almost too pretty to open. Did Babe help you?"

Len nodded.

Holding the small jewelry box in her hand, Emily hesitated.

"It's no ring yet, but don't worry. That's coming."

Emily giggled just a second too long. She opened the box and her eyes grew wide.

"Len, oh my goodness. It's too much."

"Do you like it?"

"It's absolutely stunning, Honey, but this is too much. How long did you have to save for this?"

"Let me worry about that, Sweetheart. I want you to have it."

"I can't keep it, though." She held the gem in her fingers so it sparkled. "This must have cost so much."

"I told you, don't worry." Len scooted away.

"Len, don't be cross. It's just, it must have been so much. I'd rather see us save up for other things. Len, please try to see where I'm coming from. It's beautiful. It really is. It's special because it came from you, though I'd rather see us save up for more important things in our life."

She hooked an arm around his and leaned in to him. They both listened to Andy playing a slow rendition of "Silent Night" inside on the piano.

"Len, you know what I want most in the world."

"Yes," he said. "I'll save up. I will take care of all of that. As soon as I'm home from the service, we'll get you a house full of children, Sweetheart."

"Thank you, Len. I'm so thankful for you. I'll keep getting better so we can do all of that." Emily rested her head against him for a moment while they sat on the porch swing and looked out at glistening snow. She let out a happy sigh.

"You happy, Honey?"

Her wide smile answered him.

"I sure am," she answered, with a quick click of her tongue, one of the habits that had endeared her to Len from the start.

CHAPTER 15

The clacking of the trolley, *click-ety click*, made a rhythm that matched Len's prayer on the twenty-one-mile trip to Pittsburgh. *Let me pass, God. Let me pass, God.* Some of his family didn't understand why he was so eager to be drafted. Sure, it was a dangerous duty, but Len knew he had it in him to fight—he'd boxed in front of a rowdy crowd in his neighborhood on the weekends for the past year—and mostly he wanted to protect what he loved. This was an honor. It's why President Roosevelt signed the "Good News Letter" he received the day after his eighteenth birthday, the day after his family had shared fresh watermelon together to celebrate the way they always did on Len's birthday. A few of his buddies, Stush and Zeek, already had opened their letters. They had birthdays in June. When Len blew out the candles on his watermelon that July 15, his wish was that he could fight bravely and return home to make a family with Emily. He didn't know he'd have to wait so long to be called up for a physical. He was more than ready.

"I've never seen you this quiet," Zeek said. Stush and Tommy were sitting in two seats farther ahead, but their boisterous talk was loud enough to raise eyebrows anywhere in the trolley car.

"Sorry, Zeek, just wondering what it'll be like," Len answered.

"Yeah, I'm nervous, too," his dark-haired friend said. "No one in my family wants me to be a soldier."

"Then maybe you should join the navy," Len said, with a snicker.

"I don't really want to go to war at all," Zeek spoke quietly. He didn't want his other buddies to hear.

"What do you mean?" Len looked genuinely surprised. "Out of all the crazy stuff we used to do, this can't be any worse. Besides, if we don't do this, think what life could be like. Think about what our lives were like as kids, man."

"Yeah, I know what you mean, Len, but I just don't know that I could, you know, kill someone."

Len shifted in his seat. "Well, I wouldn't like it. I never killed anything except when the neighbor asked me to shoot a sick old dog for him. I didn't like it. I didn't want to do it and I felt bad after, but I knew it had to be done. You gotta look at it like that, Zeek."

"Remember when we found that guy in the woods when we were out looking for trees for beanpoles across the highway?"

Len nodded. "Yeah, I thought that smell was a dead animal," he said. "He had his head on a rock."

"Yeah, and there were bugs running through his face. Mafia did it to him, and the police told us not to say anything more about it. I can't be like that. I can't do that to someone."

"You won't be like that, my friend."

Looking out the window at Pittsburgh's lush countryside, Len went back to his silent chant, praying he would pass the physical. The train stopped before any of them were prepared.

The brick building in downtown Pittsburgh was full of anxious-looking men. The Canonsburg boys brought their paperwork to sign in, and an army officer in full uniform stood next to a receptionist at the front desk. Len and his buddy Stush were farther ahead in line than Zeek and Tommy.

"I'll take those," the officer said, glancing over the first page. "Okay, Leonardo, here's what's going to happen. You can't leave this building until you sign up for something—Army, Navy, Marines, or whatever. It doesn't matter to me, but you have to sign up before you leave the building. Head down the hall to the auditorium. You'll see the tables set up with information and someone to answer your questions. Take these papers and hand them to the recruiters at the table you choose. Then we'll do a physical. If you pass, we'll swear you in."

Len looked at Stush and back at the officer.

"Yes, sir," Len answered. "And after we swear in?"

"After you swear in, you're a soldier, a sailor, or whatever you choose. You'll get orders in the mail."

The officer took Stush's papers next.

"Okay, Stanley, is it? Same instructions to you. You two head down and sign up."

They walked down a hall ahead of the rest of their crew to a big room bustling with men in uniform and young men holding paperwork and standing in lines.

"What do you think, Stush?"

"I don't know, Len," he answered. "Seems like it all happens pretty fast. I didn't know we'd have to decide today."

"No reason to wait," Len said with a grin. "There's the navy table. Let's join. We'll be sailors."

"No, I have a brother in the navy."

"So what?"

"He hates it. I don't want to join the navy."

"All right." They walked around. "Over there. There're the Marines. You think you're cut out for that?"

"Of course," Stush said. "I can do whatever, just not the navy like Tommy."

"Doesn't look like there are too many guys aiming for this," Len said. "We're tougher than all them."

The recruiter, a man who looked to be in his thirties with chiseled muscles and a freshly trimmed crew cut, shook his head as they came over. He motioned for them to go away. Len puffed up his chest and approached him.

"Morning, sir. We want to be Marines."

"No." The recruiter stepped behind a table and sat down.

"We're strong," Len kept on. "We're ready to be Marines."

"It's not that, boys." The officer's face lacked expression. "Go to another table. We're at quota. No more room."

The boys kept looking.

"Where do you think Zeek and Tommy went off to?" Stush asked.

"Who knows?" Len answered. "We'll catch up to them." He stopped and pointed up at a sign that read "Paratrooper."

Stush shook his head vehemently. "Oh, no way, Len. Not me."

"Let's just go ask. Come on, Stush."

Stush still was shaking his head, but he followed Len as he sauntered over to an officer.

"What's this about?" Len took the lead. "We have to sign up somewhere before we leave."

The officer gave them both a serious once-over.

"Have a seat, boys."

They complied, but Stush still looked unsure.

"How do you feel about heights?"

They both shrugged.

"Well, this is a paratrooper outfit."

Len's eyebrows rose. "You mean jumping out of airplanes, right?"

"With a parachute, of course," the officer answered.

"I'm in," Len said without hesitating. Stush didn't speak. The officer explained the routine: basic training in North Carolina and then training to fold a 'chute, jump from airplane doors, and land ready to fight. Len was game. Stush needed more convincing.

"I'll give you two a minute," the officer said. He stepped away to talk with another man in uniform.

Len looked at Stush, his friend as long as he could remember.

"This isn't for me, Len."

"No, no, you're coming with me," Len said. "Think of the stories we'll have."

"This really isn't what I'm looking for."

"But we have to sign up. You heard the first officer."

"But we don't have to sign up to kill ourselves jumping out of planes." Stush stood, ready to leave.

It was the first time Len had ever seen his friend look intimidated.

"All right, Stush. I'll tell him."

Len stood, too, and looked over toward the officer to catch his eye. He must have read their faces because he offered another incentive.

"I know this isn't for everyone," the officer said. "But there's one thing I forgot to tell you. For every jump you make, you get fifty dollars."

Immediately, Len sat back down and handed over his paperwork.

"Sign me up."

Stush let out a sigh and did the same.

—⁓—

"Man, you're crazy." Stush crossed his arms and leaned back in a metal chair in a waiting room where men were lined up to take their physical.

"Think about it, Snake. We'll get fifty bucks each jump," Len said, pacing, looking at his friend. "Think how many beanpoles we'd have to find, trim, and sell to make fifty bucks. We were getting a nickel apiece."

Stush smiled.

"Those were the days," he said. "But if you're not worried about leaping out of planes, why can't you stand still?"

"You know me. That's how I am. Nothing's going to hurt us out there," Len answered. "I just want to pass this physical. That's all."

Zeek and Tommy entered. They'd made a beeline for the Marines, too, and got the same response as Len and Stush, so they wound up signing up for the navy together.

"Leonardo Fenimore?" A nurse stood at the door.

Len continued his prayer to pass as a nurse checked his height, weight, and eyesight and then as a doctor gave him a thorough examination.

"Okay, son," the doctor said, finally. "We're all finished here. Which branch are you joining?"

"Army paratroopers unit." Len looked for confirmation in the doctor's face. He couldn't wait a second longer to know.

"Congratulations, soldier. You're a 1A."

Pumping his fists in the air, Len gave a victorious shout. Nobody wanted to flunk the physical.

Stush was grinning when Len found him outside the doctor's room.

"1A, man," he said.

Len let out a loud cheer. "Me, too. We'll be taking off soon. All that's left is to get sworn in."

Relieved, they waited for Zeek and Tommy. It was about ten minutes until they came out, looking like they'd just lost a high school sports championship.

"No way," Len whispered. He looked up at Zeek. "What's the matter with you?"

"I guess too much basketball." Zeek slumped into a folding chair.

"What?"

"Enlarged heart," Zeek said. "Me and Tommy, too. The doctor said it must have been from playing too much ball."

"You serious?" Len probed.

Sullen, neither answered. They kept quiet as the trolley took all four back home to Canonsburg. Two of them arrived home as sworn-in privates in the United States Army.

CHAPTER 16

FEBRUARY 1943 "How are you today, Sweetheart?" Len stepped into her bedroom. "Don't get up. I know you're tired."

"Oh, Len," Emily said. She started to cry.

"It's going to be all right," Len said, touching her hands. She was perfectly groomed. Emily always took care of herself in every way, even when she knew she was staying home. Len looked into her eyes. "You stay busy getting better. I can see it in those hazel eyes, Em. Your sparkle is back. I know you're getting better. I wish I could be here to help you."

At least she'll be cared for here with her parents, Len thought.

"Write to me," he said. "That will keep me going."

"Seems like we've spent so much time apart," Emily said quietly. "I thought, finally, that we'd be able to be like other couples. But I'll get by on love letters again."

"That's right, Sweetheart," Len said. "There's no giving up on us."

He smoothed her hair back and kissed her.

"Do you really believe it, Len? Do you believe we'll make it through all this?"

"I know it, Em," he said, holding her. "We're going to make it. We're going to be a beautiful family one day. You'll see."

Emily tried to push away thoughts of what the doctors had said about having a child in her condition, how they tried to make her agree to stop any life before it started in her womb.

"I'll go before your dad comes up here after me," Len said, standing. "I have to go now, Honey."

"Lenny, please don't go."

"I have to," he said, a look of determination in his eyes.

Emily knew it was true.

"Then I will have to just keep praying," she said, matching his resolute tone. "On my dresser, pick up the Miraculous Medal. Hand it to me, Len."

Moving her fingers over the outline of the Virgin Mother on the medal, Emily whispered a prayer. Len bent near her, and she put the silver-linked chain around his neck.

"Please, God, keep my Lenny safe."

As he walked away toward Canonsburg, Len turned and saw Emily, Clara, and her parents clustered together behind the living room window, waving and watching him walk away. They didn't stop until he slipped from view.

Five miles down the road, back in his Italian neighborhood, his buddies saluted as he walked past. A few of the mothers came out to hug him and wish him Godspeed. The girls all were there at his house—Dolly, Cynthia, Tony, Babe. Even Pete had decided to stay home rather than take his latest girl out on the town. The sisters enveloped him in a lingering hug.

"Len, do you really have to go?" It was Cynthia, her arm wrapped around Len.

"I wish I didn't," Len said. "I'll miss you girls."

His sisters doted on him while their mother set the table. The smell of her spaghetti sauce, made from fresh tomatoes spread out on a sheet in the sun, filled the home. It was a scent that usually lured visitors from around the neighborhood. The family sat together, twirling fresh pasta among meatballs, and Len showed them the Miraculous Medal Emily had given him.

"You'll have a lot of women praying for you," Cynthia said, touching Len's forearm.

From the head of the table, Len's dad spoke. His cheeks shook with each word.

"Len, I don't want you to go. It's a suicide mission. That's what all my friends said. If you have to go, okay, but not as a paratrooper."

"It will be okay, Pop."

He rose and helped his mother clear the table and set dishes into foaming water.

They all gathered on the porch, and their mother's eyes filled with tears.

"My son," she said. "What will I ever do without you here?"

"I'm coming back, Mum, promise," he said. "I love you." He turned to his sisters, clustered behind him. "Cynthia, I'm going to need you to take my place brushing Mum's hair for me until I get home."

"Nadaduch," his mother sighed.

Each of his siblings hugged him, even Pete. Then Len's father wrapped his arms around him. Len was surprised to feel his dad's shoulders shaking as he held onto him. When he stepped back, Len saw something he'd never seen before: His father was crying.

"Pop," Len put his forehead against him and kissed him on the cheek. "I love you, Pop."

Silence.

Len's father brushed away tears from his cheeks, patted his son on the back, and picked up his bag.

Len joined his friend on the street and they walked to the trolley stop. His mind wasn't on the struggles he expected to face or the rigor of training. He had one thought. *When I'm a father, I will tell my children I love them. I will say it as often as I can.*

CHAPTER 17

My Goldietop,

I'm a long way from home, from you. There are 15,000 of us here at Camp Mackall in North Carolina, all dumped off from the train last week. It's exciting, in a way, to be part of the new Airborne Division. You should see what our jumpsuits will look like, once we earn them. It's a lot of training ahead.

I thought about you the whole way down here. We started out at 6 a.m. and it was about midnight 'til we got here. I think we stopped at every small town on the way. I don't think I slept at all that first night in the barracks—just one long building really—but I'm getting used to this, or trying to. Boot camp started the day after we got here. Some boys are having a harder time than others. I'm telling you, I never knew there were so many ways to do pushups. You wouldn't believe it, Honey. We were doing pushups on our knuckles from the first day. They're getting us in fighting shape.

I miss you, Sweetheart. Thinking of you is what keeps me going. I still don't know where I'm headed, but I know I'll wind up back home with you. We'll start our lives together then.

All my Love, Len

With a sigh, Emily folded the letter. *I hope he's right. Dear God, let my Len come home safe. Go with him. You've told me we are to be together. I know that. Bring us back together.*

"Emily?" It was her mother who walked into her bedroom. "I don't know that you should be kneeling just yet."

"I'm getting better, Mum." Emily smiled weakly. Worry showed on her mother's face.

"Well, you've done nothing but hide away in your room since you got that letter three days ago. It'll be good for you to get outside today. We had better hurry if we're going to catch the trolley."

Emily, standing now and pinning her hair, drooped. It was the thought of the trolley and where it would take them. She wasn't sure she was ready for treatment again. She'd hoped to leave that behind at the sanatorium, but even though the doctor in town couldn't believe she was improving as she had after her dismissal from Mount Alto, he had convinced her family she needed to continue treatment. So had her persistent, nighttime fits of coughing.

"And I want to take you to lunch first. The neighbor is waiting outside with a car." Emily's mother paused a moment and handed her a few pressed white kerchiefs with embroidered designs. "He's nice to do this for us. He just asked that you cover your cough with a hankie. I told him you'd do that anyway, but make sure he sees that you have one."

Holding the fabric in one hand, Emily grabbed the letter from Len with the other, tucked it in her pocket, and followed her mother dutifully to the car waiting outside. The three of them were quiet on the way to town on that cool fall day, the kind that would be perfect for a walk down the street with her beau.

At the café, Emily's mother thanked their neighbor for the ride and they found a table outside.

"That doctor was wrong, you know," she finally said to her daughter. "You're getting better. You just needed to be home."

"Well, you're taking good care of me, Mum."

Her eyes wandered to the furniture and department store next door, the one where they sold just about everything, including evening gowns and wedding dresses.

"Look at that, all that lace," she said.

"It's lovely, dear," she said. "Reminds me of what Mary Agnes wore."

"Yes, I wish I could have been here." Emily's voice waivered. "I missed so much."

"Well, this is your big turnaround," she said, patting her daughter's hand. "We'll get you out to see this new doctor and you'll not be missing anything again."

The two rose to leave toward the trolley station, arm in arm, when Emily's mother stopped.

"You know, we have a few minutes," she said. "Let's go see that dress close up."

"Really, Mum?"

"Yes," she said. "I want to see more of that beautiful smile."

Emily ran her hands over every inch of lace on the mannequin's arms and walked behind to see the trail of creamy fabric.

"It is lovely, isn't it?" A slender saleswoman in her thirties approached them. "We had four in last month, and wouldn't you know, there's just one left. Well, plus the one on the mannequin, but that's for show. It's certainly a popular style. The tailoring is exquisite."

"This girl knows her dresses," Emily's mother answered. "I'll bet she could sew one just like this one."

But Emily didn't look up or respond. She was lost in the thought of lace swishing with her steps, a bouquet in hand, and a church full of her friends and family—Italian and Slovak—rising as she walked toward him, to Len, waiting up front.

"Emily?"

"Yes, Mum, it's beautiful. It's perfect."

The saleswoman stepped closer. "When is your wedding? Would you like to try it on? Like I said, we only have one left."

Emily's mother glanced at an old clock in the back of the room.

"I'm afraid we don't have time," she said, reaching for Emily's hand. "Maybe we'll be back."

The door chime to Brody's Department Store sounded as they left, and the way only a mother can, Emily's mother asked the very question that had been troubling her.

"Do you really think Len is this serious about you? You know, a lot of boys, when they go off to fight, need to know they have someone at home thinking about them. I just don't want you to be hurt. You've been through enough already with all these treatments."

The words sank to Emily's heart. Her eyes filled with tears as she answered her mother, both of them walking slowly on a narrow sidewalk toward the trolley station.

"Mum, I've thought—I mean, I have to hope," she said. "Len is everything. He's the reason I have to get better. I know God brought him into my life for a reason, because we're to be together and be a family. If I don't have that hope, if I don't believe it, I don't believe I can get better, either. I wish, with all my heart, that he didn't have to go. I begged him. You remember how it was. But it's something he has to do right now. He waited for me while I was in the sanatorium, and I'll wait for him here, no matter how long."

Stopping at the station, Emily's mother held her. "God made you strong, my baby girl. You hold on to that faith. It will carry you through everything and get you through today. I just wish things were easier for you."

The trolley's clacking soothed Emily into a gentle sleep against her mother's shoulder on the way to Pittsburgh. Pulling out her own kerchief, Emily's mother dabbed away tears as she rocked her sleeping teenage child on the way to see a new doctor, one she hoped would save her daughter's life. She begged God to forgive her for bitter feelings, her anger that a girl Emily's age would have to endure such fatigue and endless coughing for so long.

"Don't let heartbreak be added to her suffering," she whispered, and kissed the top of Emily's head. "I hope you're right about this Italian boy."

A child about eight years old in pigtails looked up with big blue eyes at Emily, sitting next to her in the waiting room at the doctor's office.

"Do you have it, too?" the girl asked.

Emily nodded and gave her a warm smile and thought again of the little girls at the sanatorium who would ask her to braid their hair.

"Yes, I do, but I'm getting better," she said.

"Oh, good." The girl looked away. "I hate this. Do they use the needle with you, too?"

"Well, yes, but I've gotten used to it." Emily was trying to sound brave. Children shouldn't have to worry so much, but for all the times she had the treatment at the sanatorium, she still felt shaky inside before it happened. So many girls she'd known died on that table.

The girl twisted in her seat.

"I haven't gotten used to it, and I still hate it," the girl repeated. Emily gave the girl a hug and firsthand advice.

"I pray the whole time," she said. "Try it. It sure helps me."

⌣

Shutting her eyes, Emily took her own advice on the treatment table. She prayed, and then she pictured Len, perfect Len, beside her, telling her she was getting better and they'd be married soon. This time it was her mother holding her hand instead of a sanatorium nurse as the doctor pushed a long needle into her stomach.

"Well, we had a tough time getting your records in from the sanatorium," the doctor said, after Emily's diaphragm was stretched tight from the pressure of gas. She listened as he reviewed her case with her mother.

"The doctor made very few notes from his last appointment with you. Just says, 'No further options' and then another line, 'Mother removed Ms. Lesso from facility,' and then, 'Refused to sign for tubal ligation.'"

"Yes, they sent her home where I can care for her," her mother answered.

"I see." His shoes clicked as he walked over to a countertop. Emily heard him flipping through papers and notes.

"Well, she's a tough case," he said. "Says here her lungs were about as bad as they can get in the weeks before she left. From what I saw today on her fluoroscope, it doesn't seem to be the same patient. It's a wonder, really."

"Doctor, that's so encouraging. You don't know what this little girl has been through."

"I know. I can imagine. I've seen a lot of them, too many. This disease is hell on the body, even harder on the spirit. She's not a child anymore, though. She's home now and not separated from the boys like they do at the institution."

"I guess so."

"That means now we have to get back to that surgery paperwork."

"Doctor, she's still young. She's at my house. There's no need to worry about that now."

"That's how mother's think," he said. "She seems to be a very sweet girl, and I'm not saying there's any worry of pregnancy, not for the moment. Sweet girls get married—does she have a beau?"

"Yes, she does," she said. "He's gone away to become a soldier in the war, though."

"Well, if there's any talk of marriage, that's fine," he said. "But she's in no state for childbirth. Even if she continues to improve, she can't bear children."

"But, doctor, I don't think that's what she needs to hear right now."

"It may not be, but it must be said," he answered. His tone was as harsh as Dr. Preston's now. "It would kill her. If you love her, talk to her about it. Now, the nurse will help you up and I'll see you two in one week."

"A week from today?"

"Yes, ma'am." His patience was wearing thin, from the sound of his voice.

"I thought you said she looks better?"

"She does. She doesn't appear to be dying anymore, but she still needs treatment, and it should be every week to be effective."

A nurse had helped Emily up, and she was leaning against her mother, one hand over her swollen belly, eyes still closed.

"We'll do what it takes then, Doctor. Thank you."

"Then I expect you'll talk to her about children."

Without responding, Emily's mother wrapped an arm around her child and walked her, each of them taking slow steps, down a hallway and out of the doctor's office onto the bustling city sidewalk. Workmen, businessmen, and mothers with children passed as far as they could manage as the bloated girl and her mother began the trek to the trolley station to go home.

"Well, child, it sounds like you're getting better. Praise God. He hears us."

Emily was too uncomfortable to sleep on the ride home. Instead, she thought of the dress and of her mother's worry about Len's intentions. *I'll write to him. I'll tell him about the wedding gown. When he answers, I'll know. He's given me no reason to doubt.* She folded her arms over her belly, and closing her eyes, she remembered Len dancing with her on the roof of the sanatorium, the way he always had faith even when she couldn't see how things would turn out. *I'll have that faith, too, even when there's no reason for it.* Despite the doctor's warning about children, she imagined the bulge in her belly was a baby, a child born of the love between her and Len.

CHAPTER 18

MAY 1943 "Man, I can't do this." The private next to Len paced a few steps. "Look how high that is."

From their spot in line where the men stood at a ninety-degree angle to the metal tower, rising an ominous 150 feet in the air, Len and the rest of his division could see the first private being loaded into the shaft to carry him to the top.

"Sure you can, Jersey," Len answered. He ignored the flash of adrenalin in his gut. His voice didn't waver. "Just remember your formation. This is nothing."

The box holding the private rose higher and higher to the top on a pulley. Every eye in the division watched for the soldier, just a tiny shape against afternoon sunlight. Len held his breath. Nothing happened. The private stood there, and though he was too far in the sky for anyone to see the expression on his face, they all could sense something was wrong. He was hesitating. Someone in the tower shouted, "Jump!" and then an irritated-sounding "Go!"

"Come on, Mazio," Len whispered through gritted teeth. Jersey shook his head vehemently.

"He ain't going to make it," Jersey said, peering up like the others. "I ain't going to make it, either. All this way we came. It's too high."

Every man held his breath.

There was a collective sigh as the private's body slipped from view, but he was back a moment later.

"Don't look down, Mazio," Len whispered again, cringing.

The line of men, eyes squinting up in the Georgia sun, heard a wailing scream as the private leaped from the door. His body was straight at first but then curled up just a moment too soon, just before he made a thud and cloud of dust in a huge sawdust pile.

"He musta looked down," Len said to no one in particular. Jersey, the private with a thick New York accent, answered.

"Yeah, man, see," he said, wringing his hands. "I can't do this."

"I'm not 'man,' anymore, Jersey," Len answered firmly. "I'm your corporal, and you can and will do this."

Army medics headed over to help the first jumper out of the pile and unhook him from his harness. Doubled over, he hobbled slowly away from the pile. An authoritative voice shouted, "Next!" and the line inched forward. After an agonizing ten minutes, the next private came back to the ground in the same box that had carried him up. The private after him did the same, head bent in shame.

Frustrated, Len reminded the soldiers in his squad that they only had two shots at jumping before they'd be kicked back to the infantry.

"Don't you want to be airmen? You came this far through basic, folding your chutes, learning your formation. Let's not chicken out now. We've been in the air before. Don't think about how high you are. You've got what it takes to beat this exercise. Just remember, don't look down and you'll be fine."

For weeks, drill sergeants had jolted them from their bunks in the barracks at 0300 hours and 0400 hours, shouting that this was it, that the men had to pack up. Frenzy would follow as dazed privates ran into each other, reaching for uniforms and helmets in dim light, fighting away thoughts of where they would be shipped and ignoring queasy stomachs. They knew they'd be called up to action overseas soon. They just hadn't expected it to happen in the middle of the night. The drill sergeants would load the men up and fly them out for what felt like hours without saying a word. They'd silence any man who dared to raise a question. Then the plane would return to the same strip it had departed from. It was just practice. It was preparing them for the air.

"Okay, Corporal Fenimore," Jersey answered. "But you go before me."

Len knew, since basic training when his commanding officer had pulled him aside, that these men needed a strong leader. He'd been promoted to corporal only a few months into training in North Carolina. He stepped forward.

"That's fine," he said, looking back at his men. "I'm ready, and you are, too. We'll be pinning our wings on those uniforms in no time."

Jersey and a couple other soldiers managed a smile and a thumbs-up.

Keeping his eyes off the ground as he rose, Len reached for the Miraculous Medal Emily had given him beneath his uniform shirt and moved it inside his undershirt, as close to his heart as he could get it. He breathed in slow, steady breaths as soldiers at the top strapped him into a harness and connected it to the cable.

Head down, body straight. He repeated it in his mind a few times as he stepped over to the edge of the tower platform until his toes were off the wood and he was standing in the open door frame. Resisting the urge to look down, he bent his knees and put his hands against wooden posts on either side of him. *No turning, no twisting.* He repeated instructions in his mind, waiting for the signal he knew would come from the jump master behind him.

"Go!"

This is it. This is what I'm made of.

Holding his breath, Len forced himself to jump. He didn't let himself think about the terror in his chest. Moments later, he was climbing out of the landing pile, relieved and trying to breathe without sucking in sawdust. He stopped to help a couple of soldiers brushing the pile back together for the next jumper.

"Not bad, first-timer," one of the soldiers said around the edge of the pile. "What's your name, Corporal?"

"It'll be more exciting from a plane," Len answered, smiling. "I'm Corporal Len Fenimore."

At the mess hall, Len counted in his mind the number of soldiers they'd lost that day after the mock-up jumps from the tower. *Jones, Davis, Ream.* He was up to ten he'd heard of when he noticed Private Jersey beside him, not touching his meal.

"What is it, Jersey?"

"Just the jump, sir."

"You'll make the next one, Private."

"I hope so."

The men seemed more at ease the next day at the packing shed, folding their chutes. It was a routine they were used to, and it felt mindless after the adrenalin rush of their first mock jump the day before. Folding a parachute was the first task they'd learned at training for the newly formed Army Eleventh Airborne Division, and it was tedious work. The privates who hadn't quit after the jump tower yesterday had taken their chutes to the drying shed, pulling them up until they were suspended thirty or forty feet in the air.

Inside the shed, Len and one of his privates, a wiry young man named Fultsey, spread out the canopy of his parachute across a long table. They pulled and stretched until there wasn't a single wrinkle in all those yards of nylon.

"You know, Corporal, I know somebody that can take care of all of this for us," Private Fultsey said, wiping drops of sweat from his brow. "He did it for me last time. Did a great job. Pizzonia's his name. No need for us to mess with this."

Len stopped where he stood at the base of his parachute, processing what Fultsey had said.

"What are you talking about, Private? What do you mean, 'take care of this'?"

"He'll do all this for you—five bucks."

"Do all what?" Len's hands were at his hips now. He felt blood rush to his head.

"Just fold the chute, that's all," Fultsey responded. "You don't have to worry about this."

"What are you thinking? Do you want to die out there when we finally jump?"

"No, no, sir," Fultsey, stammering now and surprised at Len's reaction, said. "He does a good job."

"So let him do a good job on his own 'chute and only his own," Len answered, frustration showing in his expression. He walked past the private and motioned for him to help fold the first flap over. They were quiet for a moment while they spread weights, twelve sacks full of lead BBs, to keep the fold perfectly straight as they worked on the next one. Through the next fold, and then another, Len was fuming, silently.

"I didn't mean to make you mad, Corporal," Fultsey finally said. "It's just that this is so much work."

"Don't you want to be in charge of what's going to save your life out there, Private? Do you think this Pizzonia cares as much about saving you as you would? Don't you want to come back home from out there?"

"Yes, sir."

"You know, as your corporal, it's my job to make sure you don't get killed—either by the enemy or by being a darned fool. Here's something I want you to remember. Write it down if you have to: Always fold your own chute."

It was a piece of advice—the kind of sturdy, no-nonsense talk Corporal Fenimore would become known for—that he carried with him from that day forward.

CHAPTER 19

APRIL 1944 After months—basic in North Carolina, jump drills in Georgia, and maneuver training in Louisiana—and then weeks of range firing in Texas and six months of unit training, the men collectively sensed it was time for a change. Impatience showed on their faces, and they watched the officers' expressions for some sign that they had been issued orders to ship out. The ones who didn't give up on being paratroopers had earned their tan jump-suits, fitted closely against their bodies, made strong from intense physical conditioning. Many who started training with the new unit couldn't cut it. They'd returned to the regular infantry. Those who remained felt superior—they had passed every test—and ready to show what they could do in battle. Each platoon had been drilled over and over on jumping out of airplanes and pushing into enemy territory in machine-gun squads of six men apiece. They were nervous, in a way, and bold in another, and getting increasingly rowdy on weekends when they were allowed into town. It was a group of men trained for jungle warfare but trapped in dusty Texas, where loose girls at the nearest village were the answer to pent-up vigor and bloated egos. Those jumpsuits with the tall boots drew those kind of women like a magnet.

Something stirred inside Len, too. He had been promoted to staff sergeant, which meant he'd have seventy-two men, twelve squads, to look after once they were shipped out to war. He was determined to protect them, but before he could face the struggle of battle, he wanted to go home and take care of something, someone. He had to see Emily.

"Corporal, or I mean, Sergeant."

Len heard a knock at his door and Jersey's voice from the other side. He now was the only man in his platoon to have his own room in the barracks. Even though it was closet-sized, he enjoyed the privacy, especially on a Saturday, when all the men were primping for a trip to town, slicking their hair with Brylcreem and splashing on cologne.

"Come on in, Private Jersey."

"You coming out tonight?"

"No."

"But you haven't been to town yet. There's a pretty girl I met last week. She said she'd wait for me. I'm sure she can find a friend for you."

"You know I can't."

"Your Emily won't know," Jersey said. "None of us guys would ever talk about what happens out here."

"But I'd know," Len answered. "And I don't want to. Emily's the only one I want, the only one I'll ever want."

"All right. The truck leaves in twenty minutes if you change your mind." Jersey, broad-shouldered, stopped in front of the narrow doorway and made a cluck with his tongue. "I'm telling you, lots of pretty girls. You could get any one of them now that you're a staff sergeant."

Len shook his head and chuckled. "Emily wanted me when I was just a kid, before I was Staff Sergeant Len Fenimore. You go on without me, but you be careful out there. I want to see everybody back safe. You know last week I had to go and pick up Fultsey from some county jail. I really had to work over that sheriff, a real cowboy—hat and holster and all. Well, Fultsey woulda been in real trouble if I hadn't come out there for him myself. You know what I told him?" Len glanced over at his .45-caliber handgun. "I told him, 'Listen, Fults, I like you. You're a good boy, but if you ever try to get away like that, *I'm going to shoot you.* Because you know what's going to happen if you get busted for running off? I'm your sergeant, so I'd have to serve your time. I'm not going to let that happen.'" He looked straight at the private. "Hope all you guys take that as a warning."

Jersey, stunned to silence, left, and Len sat on his makeshift bed and wrote to Emily.

> Goldietop,
> Sweetheart. I want you to go straight to Brody's and find that gown you liked. Get it ready, because we're going to see the priest!
> I've asked for a furlough at the end of March, and I'm coming straight home to you. When I get there, we're getting married, even if I have to jump down onto your roof from a plane. I don't care what our parents say, we are going to be husband and wife. It's our choice.
> I'll only have 10 days off, so we have to be quick. I'll write as soon as I know the day I'll meet you at the station for the biggest kiss you ever got.
>
>   I love you, Len
>
> Oh, yeah, they made me a Staff Sergeant! Tell Pop I'm coming home to ask for his daughter's hand in marriage.

Captain Cranes called Len into his office the next day.

"This is hard, Fenimore. You know we're getting ready to ship out."

"Yes, sir. I just want ten days. I'll be back."

"You have to be." The captain, the one all the men called "Chesty" because he was a short man with a protruding chest, sat at a desk and stamped some paperwork. That chest was so big it covered up any sign of a neck. His head sat right on his disproportionately broad shoulders and chest. "I'm going to let you go. You go get married, but come right back here. The army and Major General Swing have a lot resting on this new division. I know you're responsible. It's why I made you a staff sergeant, but I have to make sure you get back here. We can't have our platoon's leader heading off and not coming back in a hurry."

"I understand. Thank you, sir."

"You can fly out to North Carolina two weeks from Monday," he said. "They may have some overnight train to take you to Pennsylvania. Check on that."

The captain kept his word, and on March 29, Len flew to his home base in North Carolina and found a train that could have him to Pittsburgh by the next morning.

Emily had been waiting for two hours at the station when she could be still no longer. Her mom was sitting on a bench, but Emily, knowing the train was due any minute, kept walking from her mother on the bench over toward the tracks to look in the distance and then back again.

"Does my hair look okay, Mum?"

"The curls are perfect, Sweetie," she said. "Your hat's crooked, though. Come over and sit for a minute, will you? You're making me nervous bouncing around here."

Emily's mom was fussing with her daughter's gray felt hat when an incoming train sounded. Emily jumped up, pressed the hat down with one hand, and ran to a ramp, wedging her way in between a few others who had gathered around. When the train halted with a screech and a puff, she looked from window to window as far as she could but only saw bodies moving. She couldn't make out any faces yet.

"Emily!"

It was her mother's voice. She peeked back at the lady, sitting on a bench and pointing emphatically at another ramp to the right. Following her gesture, Emily looked across the platform, and she and Len locked eyes. The moment he saw her, he broke into a dash. The handsome man in uniform scooped her up like she weighed nothing. Cradling her, he spun them in a circle and kissed her deeply. Lost in the sensation, Emily held him close until Len pulled back and looked at her face, her beaming hazel eyes. Emily reached to fix her hat, slipping backward off her golden curls. Len kissed her and spun her once more, and she threw the hat high in the air with an exuberant laugh.

"I love you, Em," he said, setting her on the ground. "Did you get the dress?"

"I did," she said. "We had to get it right off the mannequin. It was twelve dollars, though."

"That's nothing, Sweetheart." He smiled at her and tugged at one of her curls. "I'll buy you anything you want. From now on, whatever you want, I'll get it for you. Let's start with a ring next."

"Oh, really, Len? I didn't know if we'd have time for that."

"Of course. I'm going to marry you right. We'll go and see the priest tomorrow." Then he whispered in her ear. "We'll be making love by Thursday."

With a gasp, Emily gave him a playful slap on his right arm. She smiled wide as she ran her hands over the immaculately tailored shoulders and arms of his uniform. He was as dreamy as ever. No, he was more dreamy than ever, and he would be her husband soon.

"Let's go see Mum and Pop. You have to ask him first, you know."

Finally standing from the bench, Emily's mother gave her future son-in-law a kiss on the cheek.

"You do look handsome," she said.

"So do you, Mum," he said. "You'd have to be a beauty, though, to have the most beautiful girl in Canonsburg."

Mr. Lesso stepped forward and shook Len's hand.

"Pop, it's good to see you."

"It's still 'Emory,' Len," he answered. "That's until you marry my girl. You sure you want to marry a Slovak?"

"Pop!" Emily glared at him.

"It's just a different background," he said. "That's all. You're my daughter, and I have to make sure you're cared for."

Len stood tall. "There's no one else in this world I'd ever want to marry, Mr. Lesso, if you'll let me."

"Oh, all right, son," he said. "Let's get you back home. Your own parents will be waiting at the trolley stop, I'm sure."

His parents were there, his mom and sisters crying and holding onto him. It was late by the time Len made his way to Emily's house, where her parents had prepared a bedroom for him to stay while they made wedding arrangements.

CHAPTER 20

The Slovak family, plus one handsome Italian, walked together to St. Patrick's for Mass the next morning. The couple smiled at each other here and there through the singing and the praying. Emily's prayers were words of thanks. Her heart was filled with gratitude, and she gave the priest, Father Kovac, a warm smile.

After the service, she and Len walked over to him, hand in hand.

"What's this now, my child?" he asked. "I'm glad to see you. You look like you're feeling much better." He looked at Len. "I remember you. You've been following Emily around for years."

"Yes, Father, and we're here to be married."

"That's a lovely gesture," he said, raising one bushy brow. "And are you ready for such a commitment?"

"We are." Len took Emily's hands in his.

"That's fine then. But isn't your family Italian? You're a Fenimore, right? Doesn't your father object, Emily?"

Len spoke for her. "Our families are happy to be part of this union."

"All right, then." The father turned away from them. "We should set up a time to talk about this and make plans. I'd like to first speak to each of you privately and then, if it goes well, maybe we can set a date."

"We have a date." Len tried to mask his impatience.

"Oh, my, that's a bit hasty," the priest answered, fluffing his robe, and turning toward them again. "Well, when is it then? This year?"

"We have to get married tomorrow."

The priest was puzzled.

"Even if we could make arrangements that quickly, tomorrow is impossible, absolutely. Now, go home and give this some serious thought."

"Why is it impossible?"

"Well, first of all, it's Holy Week." It was the priest who was getting impatient now. "There's no way I could marry you. I've never married a couple during Holy Week."

"Father, please," Emily looked at him with wide, pleading eyes. "He's only home for ten days, eight days now. He'll be shipped off to war soon. This is our only chance."

"Goodness, child." He sighed and shrugged. "Wish I could help you two. I just can't do it this week."

"Isn't there any way?" Len asked as the priest turned away from him.

He stopped but didn't turn around. They were watching the back of his head and heard him hum as he thought out loud.

"Nope. There's no way I can do it any day this week. That's unless you get dispensation from the bishop, but that's a lot of trouble. There's no way you could get that, plus a marriage license, in time."

The priest turned his head to him. "It's unfortunate, but you're just out of luck. Wish I could help."

"Wait, please, Father. Where do we get a marriage license?"

"The county seat, of course," the priest answered. "You'll have to go to Washington, and they close at 4 p.m. Next bus out of here, if I remember correctly, will get you there by three."

———

The family waited outside. Emily was in tears as Len explained the priest's reaction. Her older brother, Andy, pulled Len aside and wrapped an arm around him. "I know what love is like. I loved Helen the moment I set eyes on her," he whispered to Len. "I see that same look in Emily's eyes. We Lessos are true romantics. I want to help you."

The two of them made a quick plan: Andy would go see the bishop in

Pittsburgh for dispensation, and Len and Emily would take the next bus to Washington for a license.

"Let's get this done," Len said, patting Andy on the back.

⌒

"Oh, I'm sorry, young man." It was another man in robes. "I'm just closing up."

"But it's only three forty-five, sir." Len looked at the magistrate, who was turning the key in the office door.

"Well, we're closing up fifteen minutes early for today then," he said. "You'll have to come back."

"We can't come back," Emily stepped forward and touched his arm. "He's leaving for war in eight days, and we want to be married."

"A soldier, are you?"

"Yes, sir, a staff sergeant, 152nd Division, 11th Airborne."

"Airborne? A paratrooper?"

"Yes, sir."

He sighed and pulled the keys from his robe pocket.

"Well, I suppose I can't say no to one of our brave soldiers." He smiled at them and motioned for them to enter through the door he had just reopened.

⌒

Finally home, Emily and Len waited nervously in her living room, hoping Andy would be home soon with good news from the bishop in Pittsburgh. They cheered as Andy stepped through the front door, looking triumphant. The rest of the family rushed in from the kitchen.

"It's done!" Andy exclaimed, raising his hands in the air.

Emily threw her arms around her older brother's chest.

"It's a miracle," she said, still squeezing him.

He brought his arms down around her shoulders and kissed Emily's forehead. "It seems everything with you two is miraculous, Sis."

"Isn't that the truth," Emily's mother said as the whole family crowded around her, Len, and Andy. "We have a lot to be thankful for."

The whole family—other than Mary Agnes, who would arrive from

Johnstown the next day—gathered in the living room to pray. Len bent down beside his betrothed.

Emily prayed thanks, for her health and her love's safety, as she knelt within the comfort of a family who loved her. What a change from her solitary evenings at the sanatorium. *God does hear us*, she thought. Len kissed her goodnight, and Clara followed her to her bedroom.

"There's so much planning, Sis," Clara said. "Can I help get your flowers together? Or maybe I could help Mom cook."

"Of course, Clara. That's thoughtful. Let's find you something to wear, too. Maybe I could fancy up one of those dresses I made you."

"Don't worry about that," Clara answered. "This is your big day."

In the whirlwind of the last couple days, Emily hadn't thought of the wedding details brides fuss over, besides that perfect dress. She pulled it out of its box and spread it out on the bed.

"I think the bottom hem is just right now," Emily said.

"Well, let's try it, Sis. Let's see you."

Clara was buttoning up the back when their mother walked in. She sat on the bed, and tears of joy escaped.

"I'm so thankful that you get to experience this," she said. "You're a beautiful bride, my sweetheart."

"Mum, I love you."

Father Kovac was shocked the next day when Len approached him with the required paperwork.

"Here's the license," he said. "And here is the dispensation."

"Impossible." The priest's mouth dropped as he looked at the papers. He huffed. "Well, this is still truly inconvenient. And it's Holy Week."

"I know, Father, but it's our only chance."

"Fine, that's fine, if that's what you want," he answered gruffly. "But I *cannot* disrespect the church at this time set apart for reverence. I can't allow music or anything of the sort."

"I understand, Father."

"Be here Friday at 4 p.m.," the priest said. "I'll marry you and Emily at 5 p.m., and you'll have to be gone by six o'clock."

⌒

Emily stood on her toes and kissed Len after he had pushed through the heavy church doors to share the news.

"It's all right about the music," she said. "I'll be Mrs. Leonard Fenimore. That's all that matters. We'll have a lifetime together to make our own music, right?"

He kissed his fiancé's hand and then helped her onto the black leather seat of his 1923 Ford Model T to drive to town to pick out a ring at the jeweler. The salesman let Len step in a back room to make a phone call. Chesty sounded frustrated on the other line. Len could picture him running his thick fingers through thinning salt-and-pepper hair.

"What do you mean, you need more time? We talked about this. I thought I was clear."

"I'm not married yet, though. It's Holy Week so we had to get dispensation and—"

Chesty cut him off. "Len, we've got orders. We're shipping out to New Guinea in a month. Train for San Francisco heads out in two weeks."

"Just a few more days."

"You've got three extra days. Don't ask for any more. I won't take any more calls from Pennsylvania, Len. Be here when you're supposed to or I'll report you."

"Thanks, Captain."

As promised, Len let Emily choose whatever ring and wedding bands she wanted, even though they were $298, three times his monthly salary. He just wanted to see her smile.

"Are you sure, Honey?" she asked, slipping it on.

Len looked into her eyes. "Listen to me, Sweetheart. After you got sick, I made a promise to the good Lord that if he would let you live, then anything you wanted, I would see that you get it."

"It's beautiful." Emily watched it reflecting light on her finger, wondering at how her life had changed so swiftly. *It is more than I could have imagined. My life has come back, full circle, in these past few months. God is healing me and making me stronger every day.*

Len was looking at his love, soon to be his wife.

"It sure is beautiful."

He was just as transfixed on his beloved when she walked down the aisle on Good Friday, two days later. It was all the same as Emily had dreamed of when she'd first noticed the dress, except for the music. There were one hundred pairs of eyes watching her every step as her father escorted her toward Len, waiting near the priest. A song of joy and love filled her heart. It grew closer with each of her steps, with every rustle of that lace gown, until she was sure everyone in the church could hear it. Love filled the space.

CHAPTER 21

Helping her new husband pack to leave again, tears welled up in Emily's eyes. "Now, don't worry, Honey," Len said. "I'll be back as soon as I'm able."

She knew he would try, but she also knew the frightening numbers, heard them on the radio every time someone switched it on. More than thirty thousand GIs were killed a month now from combat or sickness.

"Listen, I know how to take care of myself. I haven't lost a fight yet." He stopped for a moment to kiss her. "I have men out there counting on me. Now I have you here, and I'm counting on you. You just keep getting better, you hear me? We'll get started on a great big family as soon as I get back. Our babies will need you healthy. You know we're both fighters. God will help us through this."

Choking back sobs and wiping away tears that escaped, Emily nodded and leaned in to Len.

"You have to look around for a house across the street from a church, like you said you want. Our lives will start just as soon as I come home to you."

Len tried to stay solid and strong, but it was the hardest good-bye he'd ever made. He held her for a long time at the train station platform, breathing in deeply the soapy scent of her hair. One more long kiss and they parted. He picked up his suitcase and was walking toward the ramp when he heard Emily call his name.

"Wait, Len! Do you have the medal?"

Peering over the moving line of men and women boarding the train, Len tapped his chest with his free hand.

"Close to my heart, always," he answered, hoping he was far enough away that she couldn't see the tear that had slipped from the corner of one eye. Emily waved and blew him kisses with both hands until long after the train had left the station. Her mother, waiting on a bench again, had to coax her to leave so that they could make it to her next doctor's appointment.

A Jeep full of fellow paratroopers waited for Len at the station in North Carolina.

"Orders straight from Captain Chesty," Fultsey said briskly. "No unloading at home base. We're all headed out ASAP, Sergeant. Chesty said we're to take your bags and head straight to the airport for Texas."

Len handed his small suitcase to a quiet private, nodded his thanks, and stretched before he joined the men in the Jeep. Not until the Jeep started moving did Fultsey and the others let down the formalities. Then it was straight to ribbing Len about his honeymoon night. Len brushed aside their jests and stayed quiet. *That's none of their concern.* But he couldn't help smiling, remembering the sacred gift they shared with each other that first passionate, long-awaited night.

That memory would carry him through the next few years. No longer was this endeavor about adventure. It was about getting home safe, like he promised.

A day later, the men unpacked in Texas, where the U.S. Army Eleventh Airborne Division was preparing to send fifteen thousand men to sea in less than two weeks.

After he boarded the troop train, one of the big steam-engine locomotives known for smoke so thick it made you look like a coalminer, Len picked a seat next to his childhood buddy Stush, who had become a paratrooper in another division. Stush, curly haired and always good-natured, chuckled as Len told him about all the hoops they had to jump through to get married on Good Friday.

"I'm happy for you both. You always were crazy about her," Stush said with a laugh. "Or maybe you were just crazy."

Len winked. "Just don't tell anybody."

"Oh, I could tell stories," he answered. "Remember those oil rigs we used to climb all over?"

"Yeah, I do," he answered. "I think that's one of the reasons I don't have trouble going up high. I also remember throwing a dummy down from the top to give all those folks out on their porches a scare."

They laughed heartily and watched the desert landscape move swiftly past through sullied windows.

After a moment and a few other shared tales of wild and fearless antics, Stush turned to his friend, the only one there who could really understand the charm of their boyhood. His brow was furrowed, his voice lower. "Do you think you're ready for this?"

"Sure, Stush," he answered without hesitation. "We worked hard before. This is just a job. You have to look at it that way."

Len had worked as long as he could remember, first as a twelve-year-old boy delivering the *Pittsburgh Post-Gazette*. He'd get up at 5 a.m. and wait by the big bridge from little Washington. Truck drivers would throw out a bundle of papers, enough for all of Len's 187 customers, and say, "Go get 'er done, boy." It was a year or two before Len, who made one penny for every two papers, saved enough to buy a bicycle to use in the summer. After his dad's heart attack, he took any work he could find, whether that meant piling the neighbor's makeshift garbage truck full of trash or killing cattle with a mallet to the head and carving the meat in a slaughterhouse. He didn't turn away any work—whatever it took—no matter if the tasks made his stomach churn. It was a relief when Len landed a job with his father at the mill, even though other boys might have avoided hard labor. Working was part of being a man.

Hours later, a jolt and the shriek of steel bending woke Len from a nap. When all the commotion—a series of jerks and screeches that made the men grit their teeth—had slowed, Captain Chesty came back to explain what most of them had already guessed: The train had derailed. No one was hurt. A few were shaken. It seemed a dark omen that, even before they made it to the ship that would carry them to New Guinea, the division's plans were unraveling. They'd only made it across New Mexico and into Arizona before fate threw them off.

The men stood out in the platform in a wide expanse of dust, interrupted only by a cluster of houses, and waited, sweating beneath a cloudless sky and beating sun. Those desert days were sweltering even in April. A private in Len's platoon was pacing. "See that street?" he said to Len. "That corner, there. You just turn right. I live three doors down the road there. My mom makes gowns for all those Hollywood stars." The private, Johnson, who favored Len, paced nervously near the edge of the platform that faced the rows of houses.

"Listen, Johnson, you stay right here by me," Len said. The private complied and kept his hands in his pockets, looking out toward the house where he knew he would have seen his momma.

Johnson never would make it home again.

CHAPTER 22

After a few days at Camp Polk, California, finishing paperwork and inoculations, Len rounded up the seventy-two men in his platoon for a ride to San Francisco, where they expected to find the majestic ship that would carry them to battle. He packed his own small bag last, tucking inside it a picture of Emily leaning her soft cheek against her wedding ring. *Love you, Emily.*

What the men found waiting for them in the bay was, well, underwhelming.

"What did you think it would be?" It was Chesty, puffing on a cigarette. He offered a Pall Mall to Len and lit it for him.

"I don't know," Len said. "Something bigger, maybe?"

"Now, Len, you know our division was only activated in February." The captain crossed his arms over his barrel chest and puffed on his cigarette without touching it. A long piece of ash dropped onto the dock. "They weren't ready for us quite yet, had to throw something together. These are mass produced." He slapped Len on the shoulder. "We'll be all right. I'll look after you. I know you'll do the same for me. That's what we all have to remember."

Len crushed his cigarette under his boot and nodded, watching ripples of gray water splash the seawall.

"That's right, sir."

"That's what I like about you, Sergeant. It's why I made you a sergeant," Chesty said, lighting a second smoke. "I knew you were a leader from the start. Remember what you used to tell the privates who'd be crying on their bunk at night when the bugle sounded?"

Len shot him a curious look.

"They'd say they missed their family," Chesty said. "You told them, 'You're surrounded by brothers now.' Keep that up, Len, and we'll make it back just fine."

The brothers, the Blue Angels, were ushered onto the *Liberty Ship* after the sailors and their officers. Len led his platoon from dry land on a ramp to the deck. Chesty had confirmed what Len sincerely hoped to be true: that he had been prepared for this role as protector, not just of his country, but of these men, so far from their homes.

"Sergeant, have your men take their things down the hole," a naval officer said to Len. "You'll find bunks there where you can unload. Toilets and mess rooms are in the midship house on deck."

Stepping down rungs of a narrow ladder, the men followed Len to their new home, rows of canvas bunks, stacked four high with only a foot or so between them. Len picked a bottom bunk and slid his bag underneath. No windows, no sun, just sounds of water sloshing as they left San Francisco that afternoon. That splashing sound lulled Len to sleep the first week or so, but after that, it was a constant reminder that he and his men were drifting aimlessly through the Pacific.

"We've been out here twenty-five days already," Len leaned against a railing on deck. All he could see around him was dark blue water, lighter blue sky, and the line where they met on a curved horizon. He'd come to enjoy regular chats with Chesty. Sometimes they talked about strategy, how to push the Japs out once they landed and which direction and tactics to use. Other times, it was just about life back home. "Do we know when we reach the beach yet?"

"Don't know," Chesty said. "It's not up to any of us. It depends on what the navy officers decide is the best route to avoid submarines."

The ship had followed a zigzag course, something Len figured out from checking his compass daily. Every day had become a mindless routine. He prayed in the morning, checked his compass. Then it was to the mess hall for hard biscuits and cheese. Len was so tired of cheese. At first, their dinners were mashed potatoes, the consistency of glue, slapped on each man's canteen plate, sometimes with a side of what some of the privates swore to be horse meat. After the first few weeks, it was mostly the cheese left, and sometimes there'd be crackers and biscuits to go with it. There was a mess hall, more like a small room, where there were only enough chairs for navy officers. The rest stood while they ate. After breakfast was a shower for a lucky few with an ocean-water pump and a bar of Fels-Naptha. An hour later, Len's whole platoon took its turn for calisthenics on deck. Each group of men only got half an hour, but it was a welcome break from the shut-in feeling of the bunks below deck. Sometimes the men would watch for porpoises and dolphins that followed the boat around, looking for leftovers.

Evenings were the loneliest. The men had taken to rounds of dice. Len—who'd lost thirty dollars the first day he left Pittsburgh for basic in a round of dice—refused. They kept prodding him, but he said he was done gambling for good. It took too long to earn that thirty dollars back. After day twenty or so, the men grew tired of cards and dice and instead wrote home or went upstairs for smoke breaks or a whiff of salty air on deck instead of the stale smell below. Nights were sleepless the way they can be when a body hasn't had enough movement during the day and the mind lacks stimulation that comes from variety. The bunks stacked on one another made it harder. You couldn't turn to the side without pushing up against the man above. The sounds of water smacking against the side, and the rocking—Len thought it would drive him mad some nights. He began dreaming of solid ground and green plants. Whatever waited for them there couldn't be this bad. This was a long, slow death march of mental torture—slapping saltwater that you couldn't tune out—and moldy cheese washed down with metallic water from a can.

"How's your platoon holding out?" It was Chesty, who had cut back on his smoking. The rations were running out, so he saved just one for morning, one for evening. It was day thirty-two on sea.

"As good as you can expect, I reckon," Len said.

"'Reckon,' partner?"

"Yeah," Len laughed and the captain joined him. "I've been spending too much time around Johnson and his western accent. Nothing much else to do."

"I started writing stuff down," Chesty said, with a deep breath, the kind a man takes when he's trying to settle the itch for nicotine.

"Like a journal?"

"I wouldn't say that," Chesty said. "It's women who keep journals. I'm just making a record, something for my boy."

"The baby?" Len knew Chesty's wife had their second child, John Junior, just a month before the ship left San Francisco.

"Uh-huh. Want him to know what his old man did for his country."

"Well, you can tell him yourself, when he's old enough to listen," Len said.

"Hope so, Len. It's about time for you to take your men out for their calisthenics. Make sure they're all wearing life preservers this time. One of the naval officers noticed a few without them in another platoon. I don't want to hear that speech again. I'll be glad when we get away from those officers. I'm tired of hearing rants about 'their ship.' Besides, I'm ready to eat sitting down again."

Following orders, Len made sure each of his crew secured a life preserver on his bare chest for their exercises.

"Johnson, take the lead today," he said.

"Yes, sir."

The jumping jacks he started the group out with felt good and got blood moving again in Len's chest. The salty air offered a cool breeze, and he looked out again at the same view: endless water. *We gotta be close*, he thought. The refreshing movement, the half hour, ended too quickly. Len soon was watching each man return his life preserver into the pile of orange where they'd found them. He stretched one last time and touched his hand to the back of his neck to brush away sweat. *Oh, no.* It was gone. *She'll kill me. I can't go without it.* The Miraculous Medal, the one Emily gave him for God's protection, was gone. How could he not have noticed the missing weight, the one that represented protection, around his neck? But he had felt it. He'd heard it hit the deck while they did push-ups just minutes before. Or had he? Was he wearing it when he and Chesty were talking along the deck rail? Maybe it was already a mile deep.

"Everybody stop."

The men quit talking and looked at their sergeant.

"Nobody moves at all. We have to find something."

There was silence. In his mind, Len reviewed what he'd seen in the minutes prior: men unhooking their life preservers, tossing them carelessly into a pile. Any one of them could have knocked it around, tossed it into the Pacific Ocean by accident.

"I was wearing a Miraculous Medal, Mary on the front," he told them, shouting now. "No one, *no one*, leaves this deck until we find it."

"Sir, the platoon after us is waiting."

"Fultsey, I don't care. I said no one leaves until we find it."

"Alright, Sarg." The men started searching, moving the life preservers one by one to another spot on deck. "How big is it, sir?" It was Fultsey again.

Len made an oval shape with his thumb and index fingers, something about an inch across at the widest. Fultsey sighed and rolled his eyes but kept shaking out life preservers and looking beneath them. In his mind, Len pictured the silver medal spiraling downward into darker and darker waters, lost in the ocean's fathomless depth. *Emily's going to kill me*, he thought again. He looked under his own life preserver. There was nothing.

Frustrated, he shut his eyes and heard the men rustling around him. He pictured the medal and the sweet woman who gave it to him. If she were here, she would pray. *St. Anthony, perfect imitator of Jesus, who received from God the special power of restoring lost things, grant that I may find the Medal of Immaculate Conception, which has been lost.*

"We can't find it, sir," Fultsey said. "We've been looking twenty minutes now, and the other sergeant has given us orders to make way for the next platoon."

"I'm the one who gives you your orders, Fultsey." Len whispered the prayer again. When he looked up, he saw the next round of men were picking through the life preservers that had been scattered in the frenzy. Len picked his up once more to hand it over.

There, against the deck floor where he'd seen nothing before, the medal shone, glittered in the sun, the vision of Mary in her robe, hands outstretched. Len looked again. It was real. He ran his fingers over the words along the edge of the medal's face first—O MARY CONCEIVED WITHOUT SIN PRAY FOR US WHO HAVE RECOURSE TO THEE—and felt the bumps of the Mary's robe with his fingertips. His protector had returned, had never left.

Days later, a private first spotted birds in the distance, and within a week, the men were stretching their travel-weary bodies on the beach of Milne Bay, the southeastern tip of New Guinea.

CHAPTER 23

The terrain would be their first enemy. Len could see that already. The beach was narrow and led up, within yards, to jungle forests. The trees were so close to the water that, as they approached from the ship, the men could hardly see any shoreline, just clumps of tropical green right up to the water's edge. Chesty had told Len about the thick brush, the mosquito-infected swamplands and extreme ridges. It's part of the reason the paratroopers were called. They could push farther into the island by plane and walk through to those places vehicles just couldn't make it.

They didn't set up camp. Before nightfall, they had loaded back up into the *Liberty* to continue northeast for days. They debunked at Buna-Dobodura and joined encampments that others in their unit had erected. Working quickly in a drenching rain, Len's platoon set up tents with cots for four men apiece as they awaited orders. They had stripped to their underclothes and were ringing out soaked shirts when another officer, Officer Martin, approached the first cluster of soldiers from the platoon.

"What the hell are you doing?" the officer shouted loud enough to catch the attention of the majority of the group. The rain had stopped, but relentless, dense humidity still hung in the air.

Jersey answered, surprised, "Wringing out our shirts, sir."

"Who told you to do that?"

"No one, sir."

"Shut up. Shut up right now. I want you to listen."

The private stood still. The silence settled for a moment and then Jersey heard it, a low hum that didn't start or end.

"Hear that?" Officer Martin asked. "That's mosquitoes. One bite and you could be shaking on the ground, sick like you've never been sick before. You leave your clothes on, cover everything you can. Wherever you can't cover, spread the salve from your supplies. Got that?"

The private nodded.

"Good. Tell all the new ones."

Len sensed irritation in his men when he told them they were ordered to set up for jump training again. They'd had months in one type of training or another in the States. They felt ready, and they wanted to get to the work ahead of them—some for excitement and others because they thought it would seem like progress, like they were marching their way in so they could get out, and home, faster. Len heard some of the men doubting, talking in whispers. This new division, they would say, was thrown together so fast there wasn't a plan. We were dragged all the way out here, and now they don't even need us, they'd say. He kept on with quiet confidence as they set up jump training, carried out over the jungle.

About a month into the training, a censor officer pulled Len aside and asked him to come to his tent.

"Hey, man, I want you to read this." The officer handed Len a letter. "It's from a guy in your platoon, a letter to his mom in Arkansas."

Three pages in, he saw his name, Sergeant Fenimore.

We're going to jump tomorrow, and this is the last letter you're going to get. Me and Sergeant Fenimore are going to jump tomorrow. We're going to get killed.

"Did you know they were gettin' this nervous, Sergeant?" the censor officer questioned.

"I guess. They're antsy here. We can hear the Japs moving around at night, heard shells the other night. Not a good feeling."

"Well, I just wanted you to know."

"I appreciate it." Putting his helmet back on but leaving the chin strap undone as usual, Len returned to his duties. The next day, Len went up with five men. The rain had finally stopped, and it was cool in the plane. He watched the Arkansas private squeezing his hands together nervously, talking to no one. The others ignored him. He was the same private who kept getting their platoon gigged at training back in Texas. They'd lose their trips to town on the weekends over and over because the squirrely soldier couldn't seem to clean up around his bunk. You could tell he was the kind who'd never been far from his mother. They'd fail inspection because of him. He looked more nervous now than ever.

Len edged toward the open door and let his legs hang out in the wind. He breathed in deeply and looked out at the horizon. He heard Jersey's thick accent.

"He must be crazy. That, or he's an angel."

"I'm not either, but I like what I'm doing," Len had to shout it over the sound of the plane and wind. He looked right at the nervous private. "If you don't like what you're doing, you tell me right now."

The man didn't speak. He looked down at his hands. When it was his turn to jump, he wouldn't budge.

"Light's green," Len shouted. "Go, Private."

Nothing happened.

"Okay, Fultsey, push him." With a malicious grin, the private complied.

Fultsey and Len heard him scream on his way out. Len held his breath until he saw the puff of the private's parachute. On the ground, he gathered his men, watching for the Arkansas boy.

"You feel like you're dead, Private?"

"No, sir."

"Don't you ever include me in your letter again, or I'll take you behind that bush and beat the hell out of you."

"Yes, sir."

⌐

That night, the men bathed in a brown river, clothes on to avoid malaria-bearing mosquitoes. The private from Arkansas kept away from the others, and Len approached him.

"Listen, man."

The private seemed surprised, and shame showed in his close-set eyes. He tried to smile at Len politely, but one of his front teeth overlapped the other, and he looked more uneasy than anything else.

"You're a Blue Angel," Len spoke firmly and put a hand on the boy's shoulder. "That means something. I can't have you giving up before we get started."

"Yes, sir. I'm sorry."

"Don't be sorry. Just improve. We head out tomorrow into the jungle."

⌐

Chesty handed Len a compass and a map. It wasn't past nine o'clock in the morning, but it was already more than one hundred degrees.

"Take a group from your platoon four or five miles in, then turn around and report back. We're not looking for one or two Japs here. They're scattered everywhere on the island. We're looking for establishments, and we need to know whether it's safe to move everybody forward."

Spreading the map out, Len nodded.

Chesty leaned in to him. "You be careful, Len. They were here for years before one U.S. soldier set foot on this ground. They know the area. They'll hide in trees. They'll hide in holes and cover their heads with sod and wait for a few of you to pass by before they come up, shooting."

With a dozen men behind him, Len led the way. His pockets bulged with grenades; he had his .45-caliber, too, and a rifle slung over his back. They moved forward, twisting through trees and vines for a mile, swatting at mosquitoes. They bottlenecked at the end of a constricted path that dropped straight into murky water.

"This can't be right." Len asked the corporal beside him to double-check the coordinates.

"I think so, Sergeant."

The men stood before a swamp of unknown depth, black in some places and orange-brown in others.

"I guess you're right, Sergeant. I don't see a different way around without getting too far off course."

Rifles raised, they trudged through one hundred yards of waist-high muck that seeped through their clothes until it squished inside their boots. All but Len were cursing when they climbed to shore, immediately struggling through thick brush and tangled vines. There was no bank to buffer the edge of the water and the overgrowth.

"Guess all of it's going to look this way, Sergeant," Private Johnson spoke. "It's like nobody's ever been here before."

But his staff sergeant was frozen. Some sense, a feeling he couldn't place, had made Len stop.

"Somebody else has, Johnson." Len tried to scan the tops of the trees as far as he could see. "Somebody else is here right now."

They shuddered as they heard a rustle, and the group halted, all stiff, except for Johnson, who drew his rifle, waiting. They held their positions for a few minutes, but there wasn't another sound.

"I think it's just one," Len told the group. "We'll press on, but no more talking. Just listen."

Unsettled, the group trudged through the jungle for another three miles before turning around. The rain was pouring by the time they reached the swamp again. They were almost across, arms aching from holding their rifles overhead, when they heard a spurt of shells.

"Hurry, men," Len shouted. "Out!" He helped each one up the bank. The shells were coming from the other side. Thanks to the heavy brush, the men would be out of sight soon from the Japanese soldier. Following behind his men, Len heard more shells, random shots in their general direction. Then he felt the helmet on his head spin with a *zing* sound he didn't have time to comprehend. The men were running then, half a mile before they slowed. The rain had eased and had washed some of the thick mud from their uniforms.

"What *was* that?" Johnson, eyes full of fear from his first brush with the enemy, looked at his sergeant.

Len didn't answer. He was looking at his helmet.

There was a centimeter-sized hole in the front and in the back. The skinny bullets the Japanese soldiers used had made the two holes; there was no question about that. That *zing* sound, that was a bullet going into the back of his helmet between the liner and the metal exterior and pushing his helmet around before popping out the other side. If he would have connected the chin strap before his first patrol, he'd be dead. He put his hand to his heart and felt the hard metal oval beneath all the layers.

"Let's get back, men," Len said, pushing the punctured helmet back down on his head. "I think we've seen enough for one day."

He told Chesty the story before the platoons headed south two days later. Chesty grabbed the helmet, put a finger in each of the holes, and lifted it out in front of him.

"I'd say you need a new one," he said. "I've never seen anything like that. I thought I said to be careful."

"Chesty, I tried. I'm okay though, just this headache's been bothering me."

"We'll be safer in bigger numbers, I'm sure. I'll get an officer from the supply squadron to pick up another helmet. Len, I'm sticking near you. It's really a wonder. It's a miracle. You just took a damned bullet in the head and escaped unharmed."

Len wouldn't be as fortunate with malaria.

A week into their push into the jungle, he started shaking violently, like he'd never done before. He didn't know whether it was delirium or death that was taking over his body. His head flashed with pain so much he couldn't hold it up, and a wild burning sensation moved down through his legs until his knees buckled, unable to support his torso. He screamed as shocks of agony made him convulse. A medic took one look at him, curled up and rocking on the wet ground—burning and freezing all at once—and dragged him over beneath a pop-up tent. Throwing a blanket over Len's shoulders, the medic looked at his squinting, lifeless eyes and gritted teeth, and he knew that he was gone. It was three days until Len had shaken the fever out of his body, sprawled out on the dirt.

CHAPTER 24

When Len came to in a haze, he was still under a blanket and damp from sweat or rain. Men scurried around him, preparing to press forward, again through untamed jungle toward the mountains to push Imperial Marines farther back. He still felt a raging fever from his forehead down, but as he watched the movement around him throughout the day, it purged itself slowly lower through drops of sweat until his head and chest seemed freed from the fire. By the time he could feel his feet again, he noticed he couldn't wriggle his toes independently. They'd grown together from marching through swampland. He'd heard of that happening but didn't dare take off his boots. *I won't let those bugs get me again.* Somewhere deeper, he knew he wasn't ready to see war's gruesome physical manifestations.

"Sergeant Fenimore, you're awake." It was Chesty, sitting on a bucket near him and lighting a smoke.

Len squeezed his eyes shut a few times and then focused on the glow from the cigarette in evening light. "Chesty, I thought I was dead."

"Not quite, but you had a nasty bout with that stuff. You've been out three days now. The men are getting ready to move farther southwest. Another week or so and we can set up rest camp."

"A week yet?"

"Yeah, we're about packed up here. Got the rations ready. Patrols have been out, and we're clear to move."

"None of Mum's spaghetti in those rations, I guess." Len was sitting up on the ground, arms around his knees. He forced a half smile.

"Crackers and cheese will have to do for now." Chesty crushed his cigarette under his boot.

"Dog biscuits again." Len fell back down on his blanket.

"We'll get more rations when we set up camp in a week. You had better move to a cot and get real sleep, Len. Your body's been to hell and back, and we'll be marching before sunrise."

As promised, Len once again was moving his platoon forward early the next morning. He still was weak through the legs but pressed on, taking in great gasps of muggy air. The next six days passed like twenty days—through swamp, thick brush, jungle, and then swamps again. When the men weren't soaked to their socks from mud, they felt saturated to the bone from heavy, driving rain, though at least it washed the muck from their jumpsuits. At night, they would set up quick camp—if you could call it that. Each of the men carried half a pup tent. They'd throw a blanket on the ground and lay down inside a green canvas triangle so small that the men were sleeping shoulder to shoulder. They spoke sparingly, nothing other than what was necessary to coordinate the next move through the damp jungle. The tropical trees were crawling with enemy marines who took a few cheap shots through banana leaves but couldn't stop the slow, steady pace of U.S. forces. The soggy march, determined at first, felt listless by day six, when the division came up to its first real ridge.

"Things are looking up, Len." Chesty pulled Len aside the next morning. "All we have to do is make it up over that mountain and then we can set up rest camp."

"How does that mean things are looking up, Chesty? It's hard enough getting through jungle when we're not climbing up a mountain." Len was spent, inside and out. Chesty's optimism was almost irritating.

"Well, the officers knew we were about beat, but we can't stop for rest camp at the base of the ridge. It would make us an easy target for the Japs.

We've got to go over before we can set up, but they're going to let us use L5s, those small planes. Sent for them two days ago. I knew but didn't want to get your hopes up in case they didn't make it."

"The puddle jumpers? We can't fit men in that. It'd take days, back and forth for all these guys."

"Well, they figure we can go up, five at a time, some inside, some outside."

"Outside? What are you thinking? You mean on the wings, Chesty?"

"Why not, Len?" Chesty crossed his arms. "Sure beats walkin', don't it?"

Len thought for a moment. His feet ached, and he knew his men were beyond what they could handle.

"I'm in," Len said. "My men will be relieved, and the Blue Angels will get to jump again."

The wind was invigorating, and the rain held off for once. The carpet of endless, vibrant green below was less daunting, almost pretty, when you weren't in the thick of it. As Len and four others made the first leap from the plane to wait for the rest of their platoon two hundred feet below, he felt more hopeful. The Japanese had been squashed out, mostly cleaned out from the eastern parts of the island and forced west, on the defense now. If the U.S. forces could just push them all the way through the rest of the island to the beach, they'd have fulfilled their mission.

Len pressed a stake into thick mud until he felt firm ground. He was looking forward to sleeping on a cot that night, and fresh rations and mail from home had been dropped in earlier and were being sorted as they set up rest camp. He had about marched the malaria out of his system and was ready for a real night's sleep.

"How's your wife, Sarg?" Private Johnson, working the other two stakes, looked over toward Len.

"Doing better, last I heard from her. She's about as tough as they come. Refused to let that tuberculosis get the best of her. Thinking about her fighting back at home to get better is part of what keeps me going over here."

The two men stretched canvas over the stakes and set up five cots.

"That's good. Saw her picture, the one where she's posing with her wedding ring. She's too pretty to be sick. It helps to know someone's waiting on you, huh?"

"That sure is the truth. You have someone waitin' on you, Johnson?"

"I do. I've been watching Evelyn grow since she was a girl. She lived right down the street from our house, real sweet blonde. Remember that neighborhood we saw in Arizona? She lives four houses down from Momma's. The two of them loved to talk about dresses."

"Oh? My wife loves dresses, too, loves to sew." Len chuckled. "Guess it's from watching all those movies. She dresses like a movie star. Both her sisters do, too. Maybe it's how girls are."

"Emily would love my mom, then. She makes those gowns for the stars." Private Johnson gestured at the tents around them and the tropical greenery behind him. "When *this* is all over, I'll introduce them. Bet they'd get along. Evelyn always liked my mom, too. She said she wants her to design her wedding gown."

"You going to tie the knot, Johnson?" Len sounded surprised. Though Johnson was only a year younger than he, Len felt like a father to him.

"I hope so. I'm waiting on the mail, Sarg. We've been talking about it. It's funny how you can know someone all your life, and just one day you notice how nice they're filling out."

Len smiled, thinking of Emily about seventeen, wearing shorts on the sanatorium rooftop. "I know just what you mean, man."

"That's what I keep thinking about out here, how good she looked last I saw her. I just hope she doesn't get tired of waiting for me."

Len gave him a firm pat on the shoulder. "Don't worry. If she's the right one, she'll wait."

Len didn't have to read his name on the heavy package. He knew right away from the immaculately spaced and curled handwriting that it was from Emily. He read the first few lines of a long letter and tucked it in his pocket for later, when things quieted. The men in his platoon were all busy, tearing open letters and small boxes from home. Len knew from the deli paper and twine what his wife had sent, all those thousands of miles. Before he opened it, he breathed in the smell, something that reminded him of his mom's packed lunches, the ones he and his dad would share at the mill.

"What'd you get, Sarg?"

"Think it's a sausage, Fultsey, but you keep that quiet."

It was too late. Four or five of his men already had stopped what they were doing and were watching as Len peeled layers of paper off and found an eight-inch salami—covered from top to bottom in mold. They sighed together.

"Oh, no, man." Fultsey, the tallest of the group, threw his head back in laughter. "It was a nice idea, though. Maybe your mom don't know how hot it is here."

Spots of deep green speckled the lighter green coating of fuzz. Len turned it from end to end, hoping he could find a spot the mold hadn't reached. There wasn't one.

"It's from my wife, Fultsey."

"Your wife? She knows the way to a man's heart, I guess. That's too bad."

"Wait, now," Len said, pulling out his jump knife and popping out the blade. He pushed the sharp edge through the center of the sausage and then held both sides out toward the men so they could see the juicy meat in the center. Fultsey gave a hoot.

"That's right, Sarg. Never give up."

Len laughed and cut strips of mold off the sides. Fultsey took the strips Len was going to throw out and scraped out bits of meat from the inside, licking grease from his lips. The first bite Len took was like heaven, or maybe it was just that it was like home, which in his mind were the same things. He shared a few cubes with the men closest to him.

"Man, you could sell these for a dollar apiece," Fultsey said, licking his fingers. "That wife of yours is a keeper."

Resting on his cot an hour later, Len opened up the pages of lovely handwriting from his beloved, the one he'd known was a keeper since he first set eyes on her. That felt like a whole other lifetime now, that moment he'd first seen her, but he could remember every detail of her girlish face, her friends laughing, and his heart racing.

My Dearest Len,

I can't wait to hear from you that this is over and you're coming home. Please remember to be safe out there. You've got someone who loves you.

You wouldn't believe how I'm improving. No one can, especially the doctor in Pittsburgh. I'm even able to go back to church now almost every day, and I felt good enough that I've taken my own part-time job in town answering phones at Canonsburg Hospital. I go there two days a week. It feels so good to help, even if it's in a smaller way. It's funny that I'd wind up working there after all the time I spent at the sanatorium with treatments and doctors. I'd like to think that I can offer some understanding to the people who come here. I see in their eyes what they're facing. I know what it's like to be sick and scared and what it means to have the littlest kindnesses, like a smile from a stranger.

Everybody's busy here, waiting for word on the war. I go to visit your family as often as I can. It's strange going from Slovak at home to English at the hospital to trying to make out your parents' Italian. I'm learning a few words from your sisters. Your dad had a funny story last time I was over. He said he met a guy on the trolley the other day, one of those types who's working overtime and bringing home big money making supplies for the soldiers. Well, I guess he told your dad that he doesn't care if this war lasts 20 years and he hopes it does because he's making more than ever. Your dad said he punched him in the face and knocked him straight to the floor of the trolley. Would you believe that! He said he told him he has a son over there and he doesn't know whether he'll make it back home. I know you'll make it back, Honey, but the story had me laughing. I know now where you get your temper!

We all miss you terribly. If I didn't have Clara here to spend time with me, I know I'd be in worse shape. I keep busy helping Mum and Pop with the house, too.

They're paying me a bit to do the hospital switchboard, so I'm saving that up, plus your paycheck and jump pay. It's going to add up, Len. When you get home, we can buy ourselves a pretty little house and a car with what we've saved. Then we'll be ready to start our own family. I tell God every day how thankful I am that he has taken care of us the way he has, making me better, watching over you. I truly believe God is my healer.

Here's a taste of home that your mom helped me pick out. I miss you more than I can ever say, Len. I love you.

Love (and lots of kisses), Emily

God keep you and bring you back home safe to us.

Stretching out on his cot, Len thought back to their honeymoon night, picturing her face, the gentle curve of her cheek. He smiled, too, thinking of his father, always trying to bail him out with sheer toughness. *Maybe that was how he showed his love.* He thought of the time when he was a boy and his dad tried to get him and his friends out of the county jail after one of the town cops had the magistrate lock them up for playing ball in the street. *We hadn't even been doing that, but those cops were always trying to remind us boys who was in charge in our small town. It wasn't them, it was the Mafia. Those cops were always picking on us for small-time things, because they wanted to feel important.*

His dad, finding he couldn't get them out of a few days of jail time, tried to sneak Len a hot dog. He couldn't even do that. His dad couldn't help him then, and he couldn't help him here. This service was something Len had to finish on his own. That brush with the law had made him realize that he had to follow orders, too, even when they didn't make sense. Some of his men would do well to learn that lesson.

He yearned for home—his sisters, his parents, and most of all for Emily, waiting patiently for their life to start. If she was getting better, maybe the doctor would give the go-ahead for them to start a family. He knew Emily would want children soon and would do it no matter what the doctors said, but the protector in him wanted to be sure she was safe. He'd been too close to losing her before. He couldn't let her live to beat the disease only to be lost to her dream of being a mother. For the first night in months, Len slept well with a full belly and a heart content with thoughts of life at home with Emily. He woke to a downpour, one that didn't let up for longer than half an hour the entire four days they spent at rest camp.

All through his time waiting at camp in that dreary rain, his mind kept wandering back to those precious nights with Emily. He imagined his fingers tracing her every curve, the scent of her hair, the way moonlight through a window illuminated her body. He imagined the rapture of her pillowy lips, soft and warm.

"So what did Evelyn say?" Len looked at Private Johnson while they waited for the rest of the men after breakfast.

"It's good, man. She's got her gown all picked out."

"I remember when Emily had picked out her dress," Len answered, doing a quick head count of his men in his mind. Even after a few days of rest, he couldn't help but notice the weariness on their faces and their skins' yellow tint from the malaria medicine they had to line up and swallow. That was something else he was sick of. "That's great, Johnson. Let's get you home safe so you can marry that girl." He pointed at Fultsey. "Is everybody accounted for?"

"Yes, sir."

"All right. Let's get moving."

Len's platoon, tired men and machine guns, moved forward. He knew they had a long stretch ahead of them through the mountainous regions. Somewhere beyond, after miles and miles of jungle, they would reach the beach. *God, protect us the rest of the way through.* Len patted the medal against his chest. It had to be more than one hundred degrees, and they had miles of uphill terrain to go today, with just cheese and crackers and dreams of home to sustain them. Already, they had heard shells at night. The Japanese knew just where they were.

It was afternoon when they stopped and chewed on crackers for lunch. Stush took a seat next to him while they rested.

"You had enough of all this yet?"

Len gave a weary response.

"I know, man. Sometimes I wonder whether we'll ever make it back over that ocean."

Len swallowed dry bites of cracker. "Canonsburg sounds really nice right about now."

"I know," Stush said. "I can't believe you talked me into this."

"Me? You were always out for adventure, Stush."

"What eighteen-year-old isn't?"

"Isn't that the truth, Stush. We thought nothing could get to us. Didn't know there was any place in the world like this wet jungle, though. You stay tough, man. We'll be home soon enough." Though he tried to mask it, both of them heard the doubt in Len's voice. It was time to move again.

The terrain finally had leveled out a bit, so Len's five-mile assignment didn't seem as daunting.

"Now, Private Johnson, don't let me catch you without a helmet. Hear me? It's my job to keep you safe."

The twenty-year-old squeezed his helmet down on his head and snapped it.

"Got it."

Len checked over his group, and they stepped out into the jungle. They had gone three miles and the trees were eerily quiet. No rustling, no shells. Four miles and still nothing. After a fifth mile, Len told his guys to take a ten-minute rest. He could tell some of them were getting antsy for a smoke. Even without ducking from shells or trudging uphill, the sticky mud made walking an exhausting task. It was about the turnaround point. They had nothing to report.

A few of the men clutched tight to their grease guns while others lit cigarettes and found dry places to recline. One group of five set up a machine gun, as a precaution. Private Johnson let out a sigh as he lay down against the base of a coconut tree behind Len.

Ping.

Len heard the single shell and saw, from the corner of his eye, Johnson's body fall limp.

No, God, no, not that fast.

Steady rounds burst from the soldiers' machine gun, and Imperial Marines dropped from the trees like heavy coconuts. They'd been there all along. Len was at Johnson's side. His helmet was still on, but his face was covered in thick blood. He'd been shot through one eye. He was lifeless, gone in an instant. *Evelyn.* The name came to him clearly. He could hear Johnson crying out to her. That was all gone. *Evelyn.*

Fighting tears, Len rounded his men up to return, once they were sure the Japanese were cleared from the trees. He carried the young man from Arizona on his back through jungle so thick you couldn't see sky. He felt like he was living someone else's life now. *I used to have a handle on things. I promised this man to take him home. Maybe I was only a boy trying to be a man. Maybe I don't have what it takes after all. What do I know? What do any of us know?* One thing was sure. There would be no more rests. He'd not be caught off guard again. This was an enemy with no pity. The gallantry of war had worn away. There was no cause. He saw war now as it was—the gruesome face of death.

By the time they reached the island's southern beaches, Stush had been lost and so had any trace of Len's boyhood. Like his friend said the day Johnson died, he wondered whether he'd ever cross that great ocean again. Chesty had tried to talk him out from his mire of hopelessness. They were a pair who had a family waiting for them—though Len knew the names of many family members who would never be reunited.

Maybe the Philippines will be better.

A sinking feeling in the pit of his stomach told him otherwise. It would be more of the same, if not worse.

CHAPTER 25

My Goldietop,

Thoughts of you keep me going. When I'm walking through these pillars of vines and tall grass, I think of what I'm fighting for, for families like yours and mine, for a country that offers freedom. It's hard to believe we married just a year and a half ago. I feel like an old man since then.

There's not much good to tell from the last two months. We jumped on Leyte, a mess of dirty huts all squished together. What a mud hole! I've seen things I never want to say out loud. My division and I are scouting these villages. I'm not allowed to say where, but it doesn't matter much. It all looks the same. There's this boy who's been guiding us. His name is Paolo. You wouldn't believe this little guy. His mom sent him out. The Japs killed his dad, and he wants to be a soldier. We gave him a uniform to play along but he's really helped us out. He's so smart. He found Japs down in an old shed on a mountain when we were looking for water. He's a brave soldier-man.

I have my heart set on this idea, Honey. I want to take him home with me, when this over. We could give him such a great life, Em. What do you think? We have so much love to give. I'd love to spoil him, too. He's seen enough trouble, and he's saved my life more than once.

I know you're going to be an amazing mother. So glad to
hear you are working and feeling better. Thank God. You're the
strongest woman I know. Honey, I love you and miss you.

All my love, Your Len

It was the last letter longer than a few sentences that he could bear to write
for the next six months. There was no good news to tell. A few weeks after
Len had written of twelve-year-old Paolo, the boy was walking next to Len,
both of them carrying guns. The Japanese shot him in the neck. The men
took the child's body, wrapped in a flag, home to his mother, who offered
another of her two remaining sons, ten- and six-year-olds. Len said, "No way."

By Christmas Eve morning, the men were eager to set up camp, but Len and
a couple of the other sergeants decided it was safer to dig holes and wait.

"Come on, Len," Fultsey prodded. "We haven't had a good night's sleep
in a week. We'll be all right. It's Christmas."

"No, Fultsey. The decision has been made. And I'm 'Sarg' to you. We
have to stay up on guard."

"But it's Christmas Eve."

"Doesn't matter what day it is to the Japs." Len was firm.

They had to fight off a handful of encroaching enemy soldiers in a
clearing that evening as the men waited for a supply plane to drop down
their Christmas dinner, much anticipated boxes of bone turkey. It turned
out to be two donuts apiece, though the men would remember them as the
best they ever ate. Something about desperation makes small pleasantries
imprint themselves as luxuries. They never did hear what happened to the
turkey they were supposed to be fed.

"Merry Christmas, Len." As night fell, Chesty took his usual stance, torso
puffed out and arms crossed, next to Len.

"You, too, Captain. Maybe next year we'll spend the holidays at home."

"Here's to that." Chesty picked up his canteen and Len clicked his own
against it. "Just wish we had something a little stronger than water to toast with."

It was two full years since he'd spent a quiet, white Christmas with Emily, now his patient bride waiting so far away. If he tried, he could almost imagine he heard her singing. She'd be sitting next to Andy on a piano bench around this time. The thought of Andy's slow rendition of "Silent Night" brought him to the brink of tears just then, standing in the torrid jungle, so far away from all that mattered most.

"We made it through Manila, Len. We can make it anywhere."

Len was surprised at the irritation in his own voice. "We made it through, yeah, but five hundred others didn't."

"It's got to get better, Len. Think of the stories you'll have to tell your kids. Gorillas. Panthers. What haven't we seen?" Chesty toyed with the watch on his right wrist, a family heirloom he'd shown him time and time again.

"Just wait, Len."

"Well, I'm trying, but waiting gets old after a while."

"Story of my life."

After donuts, papaya, and bananas for their meal, Len ordered the men to set up their machine guns on the banks of a river nearby. They could hear the enemy on the other side, only fifty or sixty yards away. The weary American soldiers were close enough to pick up their haunting war cry: "Tonight you're going to die, Joe. Tonight you're going to die."

Len said they could dig holes to rest, but even that idea didn't sit well with the careful sergeant. His gut told him no one would sleep that night. He had promised himself never to go against his instincts again, not after the day Johnson was lost in the coconut grove. Ignoring their complaints, he ordered his soldiers to make a half circle around the bank and be ready with their machine guns.

"Well, a Merry Christmas to you, too," Fultsey remarked in a sarcastic tone.

He heard the others, Jersey and even the mousey private from Arkansas, muttering curses as they set up.

"Now, listen, boys." Len approached them. "I'm trying to keep you safe.

Those Japs are hoping we'll celebrate. They're counting on it. They know it's Christmas as well as we do. They want us to let our guard down."

It didn't change the mood.

They sat, restless at first, and then succumbed to the slippery sounds of the river gurgling in the moonlight. Len found his mind wandering to Emily, sleeping soundly he hoped, though he knew it wasn't the same time of day there. The stockings would be hung, loaded with fruit and nuts. Fresh snow would be piling up on the ground—he always wanted to be the first to leave his footprints, before his sisters would join him to make snow angels or build snowmen. He dreamed of the scent of pine from a sparkling tree at home but could only breathe the sticky stench of the jungle. He wished for Stush. He was the only one who could have appreciated the Christmas wonderland they were missing back in Canonsburg. Christmas would be heartbreak for his family this year. *And what about Johnson?* He thought of Evelyn running her hands over the folds of a wedding gown she'd never wear, weeping. What joy could be left for her, or for Johnson's mother? He jumped up, determined.

"Stay awake, men." He walked to each man in what was left of his seventy-two-man squad, crouched behind machine guns. He gave each fellow's shoulders a brisk shake. "Listen to me. Stay awake."

By his fourth round, somewhere around 4:30 a.m., Fultsey snapped again. Len was done reasoning.

"Fultsey, no more from you." Len glared at him. "I've bailed you out before."

Dawn was just starting to stretch out on a dreary Christmas morning. "If you'd shut your big mouth a bit, Fultsey, you'd hear them. They're counting on us partying."

The private complied and then his eyes widened. Sure enough, the enemy marines were shouting. In the distance, he could hear high-pitched sounds, repeating the mantra, "I'm going to get you, Joe." Every U.S. soldier was "G.I. Joe" to them, a generic, soulless target.

"All right, Sarg. You got it."

But after another half hour of boredom, Fultsey had found his smart mouth again. It was never far from the surface.

"I told you nothing was going to happen, Sarg."

"Fultsey, I thought I said we weren't talking about it."

"Talking about what? Nothing has happened. Nothing's gonna happen."

Just then they heard an unnatural sloshing in the river. Against the first rays of dawn, the men felt terror rise in their chests as they saw the silhouette—scores of heads in the river, more than one hundred even, arms raised and carrying bamboo poles and bayonets.

"They thought they'd find us passed out from brandy," Len whispered, enraged. He gave the signal and the machine guns let loose. None of his men were casualties that morning. At sunrise, they could see the bodies floating—the ones not carried away by the current—and the crimson mixing with orange river water. The enemy had been easy prey that Christmas. *We turned the tables. That was for Johnson.*

It was another story Len wouldn't repeat for years. He did, though, stop to write a tender letter to his wife. He could sense worry in her letters. Besides that, he felt like it was the only way to feel human again. The carnage had numbed him to emotion, and he struggled against the grip of endless combat.

> My Beautiful Goldietop,
>
> When I get back, I'm going to hold you. I'm going to kiss you like I never did before. I knew you were a treasure when I met you, when I saw that pretty young thing at the game, but I can say now I didn't know what I had. After all this, all I want is to be in your arms. Marrying you was the smartest thing I ever did. I know now. I'd give anything just to touch your cheek and kiss your sweet lips.
>
> Always remember that I love you, Your Len

That night, he was shaking like hell again, freezing and scalding at once and lost for four days to his second bout with malaria.

CHAPTER 26

MAY 1945 "How about that woman at the prison camp?" Chesty crushed his cigarette.

"The one who wanted to marry me? I told her I'm already married, and I don't need the ten grand."

Chesty let out a barrel laugh and slapped Len on the back.

"I'm going with you this morning, Len. Go and get your soldiers."

"You sure? There're twelve of us, and it's only three miles."

"I'm sure. I'm bored. Besides, it's good company. I hear you do good work on patrols, and I want to watch how you operate."

"All right, Chesty. Your call. I hate patrols myself." Len turned around but hesitated and called back to his captain. "Just remember, this is my patrol."

Chesty held out his hands in a friendly gesture. "You are in charge, Boss."

The men pushed through grass six feet tall and sharp as knife blades until they reached a clearing. Fultsey checked the map.

"This is it, Sarg."

"Good, quick work today," Len answered, anxious to return to camp. Chesty seemed disappointed to turn back so soon. He peered out above the grasses like he was looking for a reason to stay. It was Fultsey who spotted the Filipino peasant, dressed in a tattered white blouse and cropped pants, running to them.

"Aw, what's he want?" Fultsey seemed antsy.

"Let's find out." Len motioned for an interpreter, who explained what the man was trying to say, speaking in great, long sentences, squeezing his palms together, and pointing behind him.

"Peanut farmer. Says there are Japs out that way at his property up that hill. They are holding his family hostage."

"Thank you." Len turned to Chesty. "I don't know, Captain."

"Five more minutes won't hurt. We can just go a little way, Len."

"I still don't know. He's off." They could still hear the high-pitched gabbing where the peasant stood, pointing and glancing back toward the hill nervously.

"He's worried about his family. You were sent out here to find Japs, Sergeant. Are you going to let that go?"

Len sighed and threw his rifle over his shoulder. The peasant led the thirteen men through a few more yards of grass to another clearing, and he was gone.

"It's all right, Len. That hilltop is less than a quarter mile away. Five more minutes. We can find him. If we don't, I'm satisfied."

"I'd say we went our distance, but if that's what you want, Chesty."

"It is."

Another two hundred yards and machine guns opened fire. The ambush was the stuff of nightmares—everything Len had prayed to avoid. Len saw four of his men fall and they all scattered, each running toward the nearest bush and dodging artillery.

"Jesus, Len." Chesty's shouted. "There are hundreds."

The two friends crouched in a banana grove. Len slipped behind a tree and felt a sting, like a hot poker, through his right leg. His body knew what had happened before his mind had a chance to process it, and another bullet hit the same leg as he fell to the ground. Another shot grazed his left leg, tearing his pants, but Len didn't notice. All he saw was the blood, thick and expanding, that pooled around him. *I can't die in this jungle. If I'm going to die, it's going to be somewhere else.*

He felt someone squeezing down on him. Still, the machine gun fire pelted without stopping. *Why won't it stop?*

"Chesty, I'm going to be okay. You take care of yourself."

There was no answer, and Len realized the captain was against the ground, using Len as a ramp for his elbows so he could shoot into the treetops. Two Imperial Marines fell onto the jungle floor.

"Dammit, I know there were three." Chesty grunted and reloaded. But, in an instant, his body shot straight up—hard, shocked—and collapsed behind Len. In a rush of adrenalin, Len grabbed his captain's grease gun and fired until another Japanese marine had dropped to his death with a shout. Len was covered in blood, his and Chesty's.

"I can't see! I can't see anything! Len, where are you?"

Len shook the captain's torso. He saw a mangled arm with the heirloom watch on the mud next to them.

"I'm right here, Chesty. You have to be quiet."

"What the hell? What the hell, Len!"

"I don't know what. We'll get you back. You have to be quiet."

Limping, Len squatted and lifted his captain's body in his arms. The great, heavy chest fought against what he knew was happening, and Chesty went into hysterics, biting at Len and screaming.

"You have to be quiet." Len repeated it, over and over through a torrent of shells, until he realized Chesty had stilled altogether. He collapsed at the edge of the grove.

"Not another one." Len wept silently for a moment and then whispered something into the lost captain's ear. "You gave everything."

Len covered him with banana leaves the best he could. A heavy rain started, and Len saw his own blood making puddles around him, bent over his friend. He looked out at a river before him and a road beyond. *I'm not dying here, not in the jungle.*

He kissed Chesty's face and then covered it with a broad leaf and then dragged his own body up, pulling against a banana tree and limping toward the murky water. *I won't be a body in the river.* He pushed himself forward through driving rain as the water rose to his waist and then his chest and then back down again. Grasping tree roots and vines, he pulled himself onto the bank. He no longer had any sensation in his legs but felt their heavy weight. With all his might, he dragged his body across and up the muddy bank until he reached a road. His strength was gone.

So this was it?

Len felt the blood drain from his body through his legs, effortlessly mixing into the mud. The heat of the jungle seemed to close in around him until he felt like he was breathing liquid grass. The ringing in his ears gave way to the alto hum of his wife's voice, singing next to him around her family's piano. *My Goldietop, how I love you. Will she know she was my last thought?* He squeezed his eyes shut a few times and opened them with great effort before giving in to the soothing, slippery loss of consciousness that covered him like a heavy blanket.

It would be hours before soldiers in a truck to carry the dead would lift his body and add him to the pile of others lost that day.

CHAPTER 27

"This is it, Ma'am. 7-3-4."

The cab driver helped her to her feet, set one small bag beside her, and left in a hurry, his tires squeaking on wet pavement.

Emily stared at the front door until she lost track of time. Since she'd received the telegram, she'd moved with urgency, without real thought. On the long train ride, she'd closed her eyes, pretending to sleep, though that was the very thing she couldn't manage for the past four days. She couldn't force herself to sleep, and though her thoughts moved in wild directions, she couldn't let her mind completely shape the picture of what Len had experienced. She couldn't imagine that man, the one who held her every dream of the future, suffering alone on a damp jungle floor. She just kept going, watching her own hands pack her bags, dress herself. It was like she was observing another woman, peeking into a new patient's room at the sanatorium, seeing someone for whom she wanted to feel deep pity, but she was frozen.

In this gentle drizzle, a weary newlywed, a woman who had not yet cracked through the first layer of grief, breathed deeply and walked boldly up a few steps between brick columns of a furnished porch, to the red front door of an unfamiliar home, one that belonged to the Jednota Slovak Lodge president. Hundreds of miles from her family, she had no backup plan and only a few dollars in her small handbag.

There was no answer to her knock. She tried again and heard only the steadily increasing splashes of rain on the sidewalk behind her. By her fourth attempt, she was weeping, a heavy wave of heartache taking over with no warning. She collapsed onto a cushioned porch chair, pulled out a kerchief to dry her face, and with a swallow, put away sorrow for later.

When she tried the entryway once more, a pleasant-looking, middle-aged woman in an apron swung open the door. Her hair was pulled back, but stray pieces slipped out and framed her flushed, round face. Immediately, Emily could smell roast cooking, burning maybe.

"I'm sorry, dear," she said, startled by the visitor with tear-stained cheeks. "I can hardly hear a thing from the kitchen."

Emily said her name, but before she could add anything else, the woman looped an arm around her and urged her inside.

"Just let me put on a pot of tea, and you can tell me how I can help you."

The woman left Emily on a couch covered with silk pillows. Aside from a shrine to Mary in one corner, the room looked nothing like her family's. The ceilings were taller. The walls were papered with contemporary colors and a design she recognized from a department store catalog. The sofa, coffee table, and lamps looked unused. Even Mary was newer, brighter, than the statue of the Virgin in her own home, chipped in places but cherished nonetheless.

"Now, dear, tell me your story."

The woman curled up next to a complete stranger on her couch.

"You don't know me," Emily started, folding her hands in her lap. "But my name is Emily Fenimore. My dad is in the Jednota Slovak Lodge."

The woman threw her hands up.

"Well, then you're family." She offered a warm smile to Emily. "Didn't you have a bag?"

"Oh, yes. It's on the porch."

"And you need a place to stay?"

"Yes, my beau, my husband, actually, is a soldier. Well, he was a soldier."

"Oh, my poor darling. You don't have to say anything else."

"He's been hurt. He's at Valley Forge."

"When did you find out?"

"Four days ago. We got a telegram. Well, his mother did. His leg was shot through in the Philippines. They haven't removed it." Emily gave in to tears that she'd fought away, even through her visit to see Len's parents, his mother's hair already white from the last time a telegram had come. The family kept saying her hair turned white overnight the day soldiers had brought a telegram to the wrong house, a message that her boy had died. That telegram was meant for another Fenimore mother. But it had been an omen, Len's mother had said over and over in Italian to her husband, Dominic, when they learned of Len's injury. Emily had stayed silent, stoic, through all of the panic.

"My father gave me your address," Emily continued. "He said the president of the lodge would help us."

"Of course he will, dear. You're a patriot and a Slovak. You are our family. I'll gather your things and you can stay here as long as you need."

Clearing her throat, Emily felt she had to tell the rest.

"Well, there's something else."

"What is it, dear?"

Emily fidgeted. If she didn't tell her, warn her, she'd be hiding something. And she'd have to go for treatments while she was here, her doctor had said.

"Whatever it is, we can help you."

"I have tuberculosis." She blurted it out the cumbersome word like it was a dirty thing she needed to spew, to purge. She was afraid to look up. She didn't want to see disgust, or worse, pity, on her host's face.

"Look at me, dear."

Emily obliged, trembling.

"I said it before. You're a patriot and a Slovak. We will take care of you."

Relief rushed over Emily, and they embraced.

"Now, would you prefer to eat or rest?"

Before Emily could answer, Mrs. Saval decided for her.

"We'll get you settled in, and I'll bring your dinner up for tonight. I'm sure you're exhausted. Share a cup of tea with me, and then I'll show you your room. Tomorrow, I'll take you to see your husband."

My husband. Emily still wondered at the word.

Though they'd been married for two years, she'd only spent a few short days with Len as her husband. Her married life had been a rotating schedule of tuberculosis treatments, short shifts at the hospital, and watching the mail every evening before a night of fitful and lonely sleep. Now, she may never have a normal married life. *But Len took a chance with me when we married.* Emily managed a few bites of a hot meal before succumbing to fatigue in the comfort of a plush guest bed with a goose-down comforter. She woke to a baby's piercing cry at dawn the next morning.

"What tender motherly instinct," Mrs. Saval remarked, thankful that Emily had offered to comfort the teething toddler while she prepared breakfast. Emily rocked the young toddler in a chair in a kitchen corner. "She was a bit of a surprise. We thought we were through having children. We just have to trust that God knows better than we do.

"You're as good as our nurse. I can tell you come from a nice family."

"The best," Emily sighed.

⌣

The facility was less than a half hour from Andrew and Anne Saval's upscale suburban neighborhood. Anxiety pressed at Emily's chest as they drew closer to the Valley Forge General Hospital. She gave polite responses as Mr. Saval spoke of all the sons who'd been lost to this endless war. He talked until his voice was simply another sound, like the hum of the motor. The sun was shining, and as the car pulled around to a hospital parking lot, she could see a group of patients, some still wearing hospital gowns and others with heads wrapped in gauze, gathered around a makeshift game out front.

The moment Emily spotted the outline of that crown of black hair, the shape of his head as it tapered down to his neck, she knew him. She recognized the flutter, the warmth, inside her, too. It was love, the same intoxicating mix of excitement and surety she'd first known at the basketball game years ago. She saw his right arm fly up, cheering on one group of men, as a player slid home in a puff of dust. Len didn't leap from his seat like the others. His chair, next to a set of bleachers four rows high, was a wheelchair.

A male nurse approached her and then ran over to Len, whispering in his ear. His torso whipped around and a broad smile crossed his face.

"My Goldietop."

Emily made out the words through the wild cries of the crowd. It was she who ran to him before the nurse could push him any nearer to where she had been standing on a sidewalk. He struggled to stand on his left foot, leaning against a crutch.

The embrace was passionate, the kisses gentle but tender enough to make Emily's head swirl, despite the group of soldiers, who she suddenly realized were whistling at the reunited couple rather than the game.

"I don't care if they see," Len said with a laugh. "I'm so glad. I thought I'd never be back across that big ocean, standing and holding you again."

He must have seen the worry across her face when she pulled away to look at him.

"It's just malaria again. I'm coming back around. The worst is over."

"Len, I hope that's true."

⌣

Weeks passed, then a month, and Mr. Saval drove Emily to visit Len at least once a week without complaint. When her coughing attacks started up and woke the baby in the night, they didn't mention it, even when Mrs. Saval looked worn the next day. Instead, they took her to see a Philadelphia doctor, one whom their neighbors had recommended, with mild alarm, for TB patients. When word of Emily's presence spread, the well-to-do widow next door suddenly stopped her usual afternoon visits. The Savals said nothing of it and drove Emily weekly for treatments with the city doctor. The first time Emily had seen him, she was hopeful he'd have better news, that the idea that she would have to abstain from motherhood—the only career she'd ever aspired to—was, perhaps, the mumblings of small-minded, small-town doctors. This one responded to her inquiries with awkward silence and a look of pity. Emily couldn't stifle quiet sobbing. Then sympathy seemed to take over the doctor, the best-dressed Emily had seen, one who wore shiny brown shoes with contrasting stitching.

"Dear, don't give up," he'd said. "They're testing new medicines every day. The science now is incredible. You may, one day, again be perfectly normal."

The words had made her loathe her treatment visits, even more than she had before. Though the surroundings—the missile-shaped tank to measure air capacity, the small bed, cold tiles, and sticky smell—was familiar, Emily felt foreign, like she'd decided she was no longer part of this pale, sterile world.

After her third treatment, Emily quietly walked with her swollen belly to Len's room on the second floor of Valley Forge. She was so tired of wearing maternity tops. All she wanted was some comfort, to know that at least Len's body was healing, that God was at work somewhere in her life. The last time she'd seen him, he was taking strained steps, still leaning against railing more than half the time.

This time, apparently, he'd made serious gains. She heard him first, in the hall, and stayed back for a moment before stepping more quickly, urged on by fury. He was dancing, still with a limp, in the arms of a giddy, red-haired nurse who had her forearms wrapped close around the back of Len's neck, as if she were the one who needed to be supported.

"You're not too bad, Lenny," she paused and tilted her head.

Emily, who by then was a few steps away, spoke up.

"Not bad at all, considering," she said, frowning. "I see you have dedicated care here."

The nurse, apparently remembering the clipboard she'd set down on a rolling table and the rest of her patients, rushed away.

"Honey—" Len was tentative.

"I didn't come all this way, wait all this time, to see you here with other women."

They were still in the hallway, husband and wife separated by a few feet, Emily's belly a reminder both of how far they had come and the longing that ached in their hearts.

"I told you before, Emily, you're the only one."

He walked across the linoleum and held her. In his room, he rummaged through a box, the few items that had been shipped back over the Pacific with him. He found the medal at the bottom.

"Remember?"

Emily let her fingers feel the cool, raised letters of the medallion, and Len recounted the story on the *Liberty Ship*. Those were the kinds of stories he told her. Others, he'd never utter, as long as he lived.

"We'll have more miracles," he said, coaxing her onto his narrow bed and wrapping an arm behind her. He winced when his right knee knocked against the table next to his bed. "I just need you to still believe. You've been strong for me. It's time, now, for me to be strong for you."

"I believe," she said and kissed him.

It would be two more months of doctor's care in Valley Forge for Len. Emily planned a surprise getaway to celebrate his release from the hospital. She and Len took a train to New York City to tour the Big Apple for ten days before life returned to normal. Len couldn't be coaxed out of his Blue Angels uniform as he and Emily climbed the steps to the top of the Statue of Liberty as quickly as they could with Len's leg still recovering. They even danced to big bands in nightclubs. It was a taste of excitement before the couple returned to a quiet house in Canonsburg, their first home together, where Len would fight a silent battle alongside his wife. The mill was shut down, so he found work at another, then another still before Emily insisted they move the next year. Johnstown would be better, she'd said. And so they tore themselves from the family and the church and the world they had known. That was their parents' lives. They packed their few belongings in discarded produce boxes from the grocer, withdrew money Emily had saved, and looked for a place to grow.

CHAPTER 28

APRIL 1947 *"Over the wall, men!"*

That Fultsey, always lagging behind. Len could hear the spray of shells, louder and louder, as the enemy grew nearer. He reminded himself he'd made a promise never to let his men be cornered again, not after Chesty was slaughtered, the day that always would haunt him.

"Come on, Fultsey. We're running out of time."

The soldier, always the most reluctant, was struggling now, grasping but inexplicably unable to hold on to the top of the bank through driving rain. Irritated, Len grabbed the base of his mud-covered, regulation boots and pushed upward as hard as he could. The shells came nearer. A glance over his shoulder and Len thought for certain he could see dozens of gleaming eyes in a row of trees behind him and then a flash of sharp teeth. In one quick motion, he reached an arm up, pulled his body over an embankment, and rolled to the other side with a loud thud on an old wood floor.

Emily was standing over him, shouting his name.

Len wiped sweat from his brow.

"We have to talk to someone about this," she said. "I don't know what you saw there, but I know you're hurting."

"Talk about what?" Len's breathing was strained. He'd pulled himself back onto the bed they shared at their apartment on Power Street. "I'm fine.

I just—I guess I had a dream. I never had a dream in my life. I didn't even know what it was."

"That wasn't a dream, Len. That was a nightmare."

Though it wasn't past four o'clock in the morning, Emily went to pour tea for her husband in a kitchen so cramped that she could cross it in two long steps, one at the head of the table and one alongside it. Though he didn't remember it awake, or at least didn't mention it, Emily had heard him before, sleeping next to her but lost in a jungle across a vast ocean. It wasn't the life she'd envisioned for her family. First thing was to help Len find steady work. If she could just take care of Len, they could find some better place for the two of them. *The three of them.* She corrected herself, rubbing her belly, bulging at her belly button and below. In the dim light, she set two teacups on the dining room table, a gift from her mother-in-law that all but covered any walking space.

"We'll get through this, Len." She put a hand on top of his after he joined her at the table.

"I know." He smiled. "You have other things to worry about. I'll be fine. I think this next job is going to work. I have another guy coming in today with his car. Maybe when this picks up, we can start to look for another place."

At Johnstown, they'd lived for a short time with Emily's parents, who also were housing Emily's grandparents, all in a one-bedroom house. Though Emily cherished their long family talks in the evening, there wasn't space there—she and Len had to sleep for two weeks on a day bed on the sun porch—and the young newlyweds needed to build a home of their own. Much of their furniture still was stored at Mary Agnes's house as they switched to a two-bedroom apartment. After Emily discovered she was with child, Len and his father installed plumbing so that she wouldn't have to use the outhouse. News of the baby came before they were ready, and of course against the new doctor's orders. She had options, he'd offered. No one would blame her for not being able to carry a child in her condition. The idea appalled her. *This is a life,* she thought. By this time, years into dealing with doctors, she knew how to smile and nod politely and rebel quietly. The doctor learned to respect her wishes and wonder at her faith.

So far, Len had worked odd jobs, starting with painting greenhouses for a florist in winter, just something to get by. That ended abruptly when the boss called Len a "crybaby Dago" and took a cheap shot. Len responded with a swift punch to the jaw. A welding job ended similarly, the culmination of Len pointing out that a coworker, the boss's best friend, somehow landed better hours than Len. Again a racial slur to Len and, again, Len ended his employment with his fist. Through all of it, Emily accepted his story with compassion and took to her knees. *Please find the perfect place, a place where Len will do the best work for you, Lord.*

She kept at the prayer, even after Len had been escorted from the local unemployment office. He'd almost punched someone in line who was poking fun at a handicapped gentleman. It was no comfort to Emily that others in line had cheered for Len as security dragged him away.

Word of his welding ability had spread, thankfully, and a handful of families had asked Len to work on their cars. That brought in a bit of extra money, which Len put toward setting up a garage to paint and weld across the street. The door clicked quietly behind him that morning, and Emily turned toward a nursery they were preparing in the spare bedroom. Grabbing a pencil, she made an "X" on the day's date, April 16, in a calendar. She had two and a half months to go until she would be holding her firstborn, and Mary Agnes had just discovered she, too, was pregnant. Their children could play together. Emily sat quietly on a rocker her family had brought and peered out a small window. She could see the top halves of three houses. Two of those neighbors had stopped accepting her nut rolls and cookies after word of her condition made it through the street in whispers. The doctor here was a somber type, older, maybe in his early sixties. He'd seen tuberculosis patients before, he had said, and he recommended that Emily, for her own sake, keep the disease a secret. Emily had been happy to find another patient there, Phyllis, a newlywed who spent most of her days in bed. They would share Emily's nut rolls, which had become as well-known as her capacity for listening. Emily had been to see Phyllis a few times. Because Phyllis sometimes was too tired to open her eyes, her husband Rudy took care of their house. It was an offhand comment from Phyllis, who wanted to be a mother herself, that wounded Emily more than anything the doctor or neighbors had said.

"Do you think our children will have it, too?"

It was the first time the image had shaped in Emily's mind—that of Emily standing beside her own child in a white-walled treatment room. As much as she tried, she couldn't purge the thought. This time, when she looked at patches of animal figures on a pastel green blanket in a bassinet, she prayed it out of her mind.

"Lord, take this from me. Take this thought, this disease, take it all away."

She spoke the words aloud over and over until she felt muscles clinching in her cheeks and then release. A warmth spread around her. Her hands dropped to her sides and she felt wetness on the cushion beneath her.

God, no. It's not time. She breathed deeply. *Maybe this is something else.*

She looked around for her teacup and found it, undisturbed, on a box of baby supplies, unpacked. When she stood, she felt the slipping between her legs—warm fluid—not blood but water. *Dear Jesus, no, please.*

Though she'd seen the calendar minutes before, she instinctively picked it up once more and counted again, frantic. She was six-and-a-half months along. Two-and-a-half months behind.

On her second scream from the front door, Len appeared in the opening of his garage across the street, wiping his hands and casting down a rag at the sight of her expression. A neighbor ran to phone a doctor as they hastily added to a small bag tiny clothes and cloth diapers beside a set of nightgowns for Emily.

"What else did he say to bring?"

Emily lay on their bed, her low back already squeezing with a slowly increasing ache. "Len, I don't know. It isn't time yet. I don't even know what he said. This isn't supposed to be happening yet."

Then she pointed to her nightstand.

"My rosary, too, Len."

Mary Agnes, dressed in a pressed skirt suit from work, stood next to Emily, sweating with agony in the hospital bed.

"Pray with me, Sis." Emily whispered, between contractions. "If something happens, tell Len I love him."

"Nothing like that will happen," Mary Agnes answered, kissing her sister's forehead and ignoring a worried look from a nurse. Emily looked over at the nurse checking her blood pressure.

"Is the baby going to be okay?" Emily gasped.

The woman turned away.

"The doctor will be in soon."

Sitting in a waiting room, Len held his head in his hands. This rule that he couldn't be by his wife's side made no sense. Another father-to-be was pacing and smoking, clutching a box of cigars under his right elbow. Len heard him give a joyous hoot when a nurse came to share good news. Len tried to tune it out. He wanted to be that exuberant man, but he knew, even if the baby somehow lived at first, it likely was too small to exist for long outside its mother's womb. This was a harsh world for a new life, born at the wrong time. And if Emily died, was it his fault? She insisted on a baby, but maybe they should have waited until she was healthier.

Emily would pray. She is praying right now, he told himself. He prayed along with her.

God, I asked you once before to let her live. I promised I'd give her anything she wants, if you'd just let her live. Len choked back tears, struggling against guilt and heartache. *I was supposed to be her protector.* They had come so far, too far to lose her here in the delivery room. *I'm asking you again. Let her live, please. I make the same promise. I'll be the best father to my child. Please, just let them both live.*

He glanced up at a clock. It had been three hours, waiting here. Nothing so far.

Another hour passed. Len pressed his hands together, trying to rub away car paint. He sneaked around the waiting room door and paused but saw only an empty hallway, and then he heard his wife's cries. Instinct called him to her.

A nurse, emerging from another room, urged him away, pursing her lips. "You can't help her, sir. You have to wait out there." She gestured to the waiting room behind him. The stench of an ashtray turned his stomach, and he stepped out into the spring afternoon, overcast but not as cold as the previous weeks. Emily loved the birds that came out this time of year. She'd watch them from her window in the apartment. He could see a few of them in tree branches just starting to bud with new life. He remembered Emily talking about how God takes the time to look after the birds, and he wondered whether he'd been the attentive, loving husband he aspired to be.

He'd hoped to see a nurse looking for him back in the waiting room. Leaning against the door to the hallway, he heard a baby's cry. Not his, a nurse assured him, irritation in her voice as she ushered him out of the hallway again. Back to the hard chairs, Len bent over his knees to pray for another hour. His throat was parched. *Why is this all I can do?*

Finally, the door swung open. Len could sense a nurse's gaze, waiting for his attention. He was afraid to look at her face, to read what it would tell him. Both fists still clenched, he looked into her eyes. They were cool, detached, gave nothing away.

"Mr. Fenimore?"

He nodded.

"She's still alive." She gave a weak smile.

"Emily?"

"Both, actually, right now. The doctor thought you should see the baby quickly, in case."

⌒

The words made him nauseated. He absorbed them silently as he followed the nurse down a narrow hallway, passing the happy father he'd seen before on his way. He had a cigar clenched between his molars. *She. It's a girl.* Len thought. *God, let my girls live.*

"Sweetheart." He rushed to his wife, who was holding a set of tiny fingers between her thumb and pointer. Nestled in a fold of blankets, Len saw the infant face, lips pursed and eyes facing Emily.

"Len, we did it." Emily, already changed out of a blood-soaked gown, pushed back the blanket to show a scalp covered in wispy, dark hair. "She's angelic."

For a moment, Len was more perplexed than stunned. This living thing, so small. Could you really call her a baby?

Then he held her.

Overcome with wonder, every other thought fell away. This new person, the smallest he'd ever seen, was the most beautiful creature in the world. He touched the wrinkled fingers, too small to wrap all the way around Len's pinkie. Remembering a promise he'd made, Len pressed his cheek to the infant's forehead and whispered, "I love you."

The doctor put a hand on Len's shoulder.

"Yes, you did it," he said. "This is a milestone. But I have to be honest with the both of you. She's very small—three pounds, fifteen ounces. She's not even four pounds. Her lungs are not wholly developed. There are a host of complications that come with a premature baby."

He stopped talking when he saw the young family, cooing at the baby, far too light in her father's arms. He chuckled to himself at a thought: *Well, they've never listened to me before.* A smile crossed the doctor's face when he thought of this Emily, who encouraged other TB patients with her spirit alone. He ordered a nurse to prepare a room with a bassinet. This patient would be here for a longer stay. Against what he'd learned in medical school, though, he expected both mother and daughter to leave his care—the young mother hopeful, if not exactly healthy.

Two hours later, a half hour before his shift would be finished, the doctor changed his mind. His brief brush with faith succumbed to his knowledge of medicine. A few of his other patients had babies who survived, but this was far too much. It was his duty as a doctor to be honest, he told himself. He put together the numbers, the figures and facts, in his head—three pounds and fifteen ounces, underdeveloped lungs, and then there was the worst thing, the one he had warned the Fenimores was the most likely, and the most life-threatening.

He charged into the quiet room.

"It's better to talk about this now, before you get to be more attached."

"Doctor, can it wait until tomorrow, until we've had a good night's rest?" Len was frustrated at the intrusion. Emily's face was puffy still, and she was looking down at the baby they had named Mary Lynn—a nod to both their mothers and Len and a gesture of respect to the Virgin Mary. Mary Lynn slept peacefully, both hands curled under her chin.

"I'm sorry to say it can't wait."

Emily raised weary eyelids and offered the doctor a moment to speak.

"Considering the situation, I think you should say your good-byes to the infant." His voice was sharp, anticipating fierce, unreasonable argument.

Instead, they were speechless.

"We could take *it* now," he continued, taking advantage of the silence. "It would be easier, better, for you all."

"You will not." Len nearly spat the words.

"That's your choice, I suppose. But she will die." The doctor pointed to the baby. "Her tests are finished: That infant is positive for tuberculosis."

But the scare tactic fell entirely flat. Words that days before would have shaken them had no effect. Emily and Len had seen new life spring from impossible circumstances on the wings of faith alone. Both felt their greatest trials were behind them. There would be more, certainly, but they had experienced God that day. They would need only to remember that gift of light, born of faith and love.

CHAPTER 29

AUGUST 1949 Len's hands were cold, sticky, clammy.

It was August, but he shook with chills, the same as he had each morning for a week. It lasted the first hour or so he spent working on cars in his garage. As long as he went outside for fresh air once an hour, he could make it through a day. Business had picked up, enough that he and Emily were able to make ends meet, as long as he took on a few odd jobs in the evening here and there. This was no time for him to take a break from work.

The girls—there were two now—were growing, and Emily was expecting again, already. The family doctor, the one they found after the experience with Mary Lynn, no longer gave Emily trouble about wanting children. In fact, her caring and stunned physician had a theory that the babies pushed her lungs upward and gave them the same rest—or even better because it lasted months longer—than those dangerous treatments ever did. But Emily knew it was a pure gift from God that was healing her through her purpose: to be a mother. It had been two years since Emily had to lie on a gurney in a treatment room or feel the long needle push into her back or belly. For that, Len was thankful, though he had wished they were further along, or better along, than this by now. They still lived in that cramped apartment, and Emily had fallen in love with a dilapidated, two-story house the moment she walked through the door. It was near the river, across from a church. The whole house had to be lifted off its foundation and moved closer to the street to make room for a backyard. Then a new basement would need to be dug, one wheelbarrow full of dirt at a time. And the contractor lagged behind.

Today, the wave of nausea in Len's gut lingered longer. He felt his stomach squeeze as he bent over an old Chevy and had to set down his welder and run for home. Emily looked at him with concern and pulled Mary Lynn from his legs as he made his way to the restroom in their apartment. She handed him a cool, wet towel for his face and picked out a fresh shirt, one she had tailored herself late at night.

"Still not feeling better, Honey?"

"I'll be fine," he said, reaching for Mary Lynn and giving one of her rosy cheeks a kiss.

"Okay, Len. Let me know if you need anything." She leaned over for a quick kiss and took Mary Lynn back to the baby's room, where Andrea had started to cry when she heard him speak.

"Be back for dinner."

When Len returned, he saw a cream-colored Ford hardtop parked in front of his garage, the motor still running. A gentleman in a pressed navy suit tapped on his steering wheel impatiently in the driver's seat, and a woman in a bright pink scarf and sunglasses pouted her lips into a small compact on the passenger's side. The man leaned out as Len walked to the front of his shop.

"I was just about to leave, didn't see anybody."

"Sorry about that. What can we do for you?"

"Are you Len?"

He nodded, feeling refreshed from the jaunt across the street.

"Okay, then," the man said as he crumpled up a slip of paper and tossed it onto the sidewalk. "My cousin said this is the best place to get this scratch fixed up. We're from L.A., visiting family here. This is just an old car we keep in Pennsylvania for visits, but I still don't like the site of this mark. Not sure how we got it, but I guess those things happen." He stepped out of his car and pointed, squinting in midday sun, to a faint, two-inch scratch. "Right here. See it?"

The man stopped to look at Len. He kept looking.

"I see that, sir." Len felt his gaze. "I can fix that, no problem."

"Can you turn to the side? What was the name? Oh, Len. That's right." Awkwardly, Len complied. He wasn't sure what this man was selling.

"Good profile, too. Barb, come and have a look."

Len stepped back as the pink lady opened her door.

"Don't worry, son." The man buttoned his jacket, told Len his name, and then shook his hand.

"I'm Roger Jorgensen. Have you heard of me?" The man looked hopeful but wasn't surprised when Len shook his head. "Well, I'm not a star myself, but I'm a star-maker." By then, his wife or girlfriend was standing near Len and nodding approvingly. "Perry Como. There's a name you know."

"I'm from Canonsburg," Len answered, straightening himself. "Perry used to cut my hair. I always thought he was a much better barber than he was a singer."

The three laughed together.

"And you've got a good personality to go with those good looks. Who would have thought? Right here in Johnstown, PA. You could be the next big face on screen, you know."

"Oh, no, sir. I'm just a welder and a father."

The Hollywood man brushed off Len's comment like a speck of lint on his sleeve.

"Forget that. You could be in the movies. What kind of movies do you watch?"

Len was grinning and gave a quick response: "Cowboy."

"Westerns it is! All right, Cowboy. Do you think you could get this scratch taken care of this afternoon? That's good. I'll take Barbie to a shop so she doesn't have to wait in the garage. You and I can talk about your bright future in motion pictures when I get back."

Len chuckled, but Roger persisted.

"I'm dead serious, son. You don't want to pass up an opportunity like this." He gestured at the buildings around him, the mountains behind him.

"You could walk away from all of this. You could live in Hollywood, living the big life, be rich and famous."

"All right, sir. I'll consider it. I thank you. I can get you in at 3 p.m."

"That's real good, son. See you soon."

The man argued until he was irritated and red-faced that afternoon, but he left Len a business card on fine stationery and promised he'd "swing by" in a few days, before they left town, to get a final answer. Len finally offered to consider it, if only to shoo the man out the door before dinner. He had only two hours between then and when he had promised to be down the road to help paint a house. And he wanted to check the slow progress on the new house on Chestnut. The contractor seemed to fall further behind every day. Tired, still somewhat nauseated, Len stepped into the small apartment where Emily—tears slipping down her cheeks—was trying to soothe a shrieking infant.

"What is it?"

"I don't know, Len. She's been fussy all day." Emily dabbed at spit-up on her shoulder with a kitchen rag as Len held Andrea.

"Should we call Doc Westerly?"

"I hope she's just teething."

"Well, if she's crying all day, maybe we ought to call the doctor or at least do *something*." He grimaced at the piercing sound.

Sensing the edge in Len's voice, Emily put her hand on his arm and took the baby back.

"It's okay, Honey. We'll give it another day or so."

Emily put the infant in a crib and closed the door most of the way to stifle the sound. Len was bouncing Mary Lynn on his lap, sitting at the kitchen table while Emily scooped hot soup out of a pot on the old stove.

"I'm going to stop at the house tonight. We'll see if that Denny's gotten anywhere since last week. I want that foundation fixed *this* month. Neighbor told me he thinks that guy may have a drinking problem. He's got to get on it, get it together. I want to be in there soon."

"I hope so, Len."

Squeezing Mary Lynn's hand, he paused to pray with his wife, then turned to her.

"You know, we didn't have to pick that place."

"But, Len, when I saw it, I knew." She put a hand on his forearm. "I know it's trouble, but it will be perfect for our family. The porch out front, the water nearby, the church across the street. You'll see."

"I hope you're right. And I hope you're happy."

Emily winced, hurt.

"I'm always happy with you, Len. I love you."

"I'm sorry. I'm always happy with you, too, Honey. I'm just tired. And there's still work to do tonight." Though he felt guilty about it, Len didn't mention the Hollywood couple. He didn't know why. *It doesn't matter*, he told himself as he dressed for his second job that evening. With a quick glance in the apartment's single mirror, he wondered whether that Hollywood man had any idea what he was talking about anyway. When he came back in the dark, he could hear the baby screaming from the road.

Emily approached as soon as Len stepped into the doorway.

"Did you stop at the house on Chestnut Street?"

Len heaved a sigh.

"Yup."

"Was Denny there?"

"He sure was there. He was passed out in the backyard, drunk as a skunk."

"Oh, no. I guess he didn't finish the foundation." Emily let her body drop into a kitchen chair.

"Didn't do a thing."

Andrea cried herself to sleep around midnight, and Emily sneaked into bed, trying not to disturb Len. He turned toward her. From the hallway light, he could see her weary expression.

"Goodnight, Honey," Emily said when she saw he was awake.

Len was moved by the gentleness in her voice, even after a day of looking after a fussing baby and ill husband.

With his elbow propped beneath him, he whispered the story about the pair from Hollywood.

"What do you think, Em?"

"They're not telling you anything that I don't already know. I always told you you're handsome." She reached in the dark to hold him close, longing to feel his hot body next to her.

"Do you think I should give it a try?"

Emily was quiet for a moment.

"I would have to stay here. My family is here. They're right across the street, ready to help us whenever we need them. I thought we were making our life together. You know a lot of those Hollywood people get divorced. You do what you want, though, Honey."

Without responding, Len rolled aside and closed his eyes, his thoughts swirling almost as much as his stomach had been that morning. Emily tried to sleep beside him.

He woke in a cold sweat.

Three days later, the talent agent was waiting on the sidewalk outside his garage, smoking a cigarette and leaning against his car. For five minutes, Len had been watching him grow impatient, stroking his hair, tapping his feet. Then he walked right in to the shop.

"This is it, Cowboy. I hope you've made the right call."

Len said nothing.

"You don't want to spend your life like this, do you? Toiling away in some garage in some nobody town in Pennsylvania."

Finally standing, Len shook the man's hand.

"Sir, thank you for the opportunity. I just can't accept."

He was baffled.

"But I can make you a star, Len."

"I love my family."

"Is that all you want from life, though?"

"It's everything I want."

That evening, he and Emily left the girls with Mary Agnes and visited the home on Chestnut Street. It was true, they found, with a look around, that the contractor had done nothing, even though they'd given him more than half their savings.

"It's a mess." Len pressed his hands against his forehead. Then he looked at his wife. She was sitting on the second of four crumbling steps that led to a slumping porch. Her face was in her hands, and she was sobbing.

"Sweetheart, I'm sorry. It will be okay, Love."

She leaned onto his shoulder.

"Look up," Len said.

Emily dried her face on her sleeve and raised her head. The street was quiet, and a candle shone in each window of the other houses. A deep blue sky, dotted with stars, provided a canopy for the hillside in the back. Lamplight flickering in the windows filled them with renewed hope.

"This is what we'll see from our porch when the house is finished. And it will be finished. My dad sent a letter. He's going to come help. We'll do it, whatever it takes. I made a promise to God that I would take care of you, give you whatever you wanted. We'll live here, right across from a church. This will be our new home."

Emily looked at his eyes.

"Are you sure this is what you really want, Len? After all this—"

He grabbed her and drew her close to him.

"I never wanted you more, Emily. I choose you. I love you and our beautiful girls."

The next day, they did ring the family doctor, Doc Westerly, for a house call, but not for Andrea. Len was in bed, groaning, with a puffy body and bulging eyes. He couldn't eat or even drink water. This wasn't the shaking of malaria, Len assured her, but it frightened Emily just the same. The worried doctor, fidgeting with his small glasses, made phone calls from a shop down the street and kept watch over Len until they knew the cause: poisoning from paint in the shop. It would be weeks until he was well enough to stand again. Len was in a hurry to get back to work. He already had a backlog of cars waiting across the street.

"I've already lost too many customers," Len argued with his wife in the kitchen.

"You can't breathe in those terrible fumes anymore, Len," she said. "You're done with that job. Go to U.S. Steel. You're a good welder, Honey, and there's solid work there, away from the paint, away from the odd jobs."

Emily whispered a prayer as he walked out the door. When he returned, he was an A-1 welder, told to report the next morning, ready for the job that would lift the Fenimore family up. The company had two rules: no fighting and no stealing. Len resolved to make this job work.

CHAPTER 30

DECEMBER 1967 When Emily shut the front door behind her, she heard the *ping* of pistols and the drawl of John Wayne's voice. The TV flashed in the dark room and lit the faces of her family—all ten of her children curled in one way or another around their father on the living room couch and on blankets and pillows on the floor.

"How was church, Honey?" Len looked like he wanted to stand, to reach for her, but elbows, legs, and sleepyheads held him down.

"Almost ready for Christmas Eve Mass," Emily whispered back with a smile.

"What about choir practice?"

"Wait until you hear the song we added, 'Oh, Holy Night.' You're going to love it."

One by one, he carried each limp body—smallest to the oldest, Mary Lynn—past the piano and then the twinkling evergreen that took up a third of the living room floor space and up narrow steps to three bedrooms. He tucked each one in bed with a kiss on the cheek and said, "Daddy loves you, Honey." He found Emily in the kitchen, fussing over blue and pink satin angel costumes for the school's Christmas Cantata, the culmination of weeks of practice. The popcorn balls and six-packs of chocolate candies from the company Christmas party were lined up in order on the counter.

"There are more than ten costumes there, Sweetheart."

Emily smiled. "How were they tonight?"

"Missing their mother, but we got by. I don't know how you do it."

Emily heard that often. People would ask, marvel, at how she cared for ten children, how she raised a family and fought tuberculosis at the same time. It wasn't even a wonder to her anymore. The day the doctor called to say she had been cleared of TB, she was calm. "I truly believe God healed me," she would say that day for the first of many times. To her, the supernatural world wasn't far, or even separated, from the one you could see with your eyes. By the time the cure for tuberculosis had reached Johnstown, she'd already tested negative for TB. A miracle, just one of many Emily held in her heart. She looked at her husband, loving him more than ever.

"I can do it because God, and you, are with me." She pressed her cheek to his chest.

Len held her and swirled her around the kitchen once or twice in a slow dance, ending in an embrace. They kissed.

"Are you happy, Sweetheart?"

"I sure am."

⤙⤚

Len slept that night while Emily prepared for the next day. She chopped vegetables for soup, squeezed containers into the refrigerator, and gathered the ingredients for Chrissy's cake, debating whether to bake it now, at midnight, so that it would be done before the house was filled with dozens of neighbors to celebrate. She curled up with tea next to her bedroom window, past the room where the boys slept, while the warm vanilla scent filled the quiet house. A powdered-sugar snow fell softly from the sky and reminded her of the snow globe Sharon loved to shake. Len slept contentedly. By the time she pulled the puffed cake from the oven, she had made her decision. Chrissy, the meekest of all her angels, would be the one to tell their story.

⤙⤚

The house was filled with laughter and chatter so loud the next afternoon, you had to shout to carry out a conversation. Emily kept her eye out for her daughter, the shy one, and knew she could find her near Len whenever she lost track. When the eight candles were lit on her birthday cake, Len had to scoop her up from behind his legs. She buried her head, full of loose curls, into her father's neck as the kitchen-for-ten filled with singing from dozens of family members and neighborhood kids—the ones who came together for three-day street dances and who knew that the Fenimores' house, the one right in the middle of Cambria City, was open to anyone.

"Chrissy, we love you." Emily rubbed the child's back, and she peered out at her mother.

"Make a wish and blow out your candles, Sweetie," Len told her, and she obeyed but quickly turned back to her father's arms.

They were passing around slices of cake when they heard bells, too early for Christmas Eve Mass. The crowd filed out of the kitchen and onto the other gathering place, the porch that faced the church across the street.

"Smart idea," one of the neighbor moms remarked. "The flowers are already there. The decorating would be done."

The group watched as visitors, wearing their finest dresses and shiniest boots beneath their wool overcoats, made two rows outside the heavy church doors. Finally, a lacy bride emerged, holding a bouquet of poinsettias in one hand and her new husband's hand in the other. Her veil was thrown back to reveal a rapturous smile and a crown of silken hair. The crowd threw rice, and the group on the porch cheered, all except for the boys, who already were absorbed in rounds of snowball fights on the patch of yard between the house and playground. Emily eyed her daughters, leaning over the porch railing alongside the neighbors. The girls were sighing about the bride's gown and veil.

The next day, after the whirlwind of Christmas morning—a living room floor completely covered in red, green, and gold gift wrap—and then a visit from a charming Santa Claus (Emily's father), the house was unusually quiet. A light but steady snow drew most of the children outside with their father and grandfather, and Emily found herself with Chrissy, warming her hands around a cup of hot cocoa after a snowball fight. Her cheeks still were bright pink, stinging from the cold.

"What did you think of that wedding?"

The girl smiled, showing the gap from her missing front teeth, the tips of new ones just pushing through.

"Mum, it was beautiful. I can't wait to get married like that. Thanks for having my birthday party and making my favorite apple cake."

Emily squeezed her little one on the chair, a reminder of God's most generous gifts.

"Can you come upstairs with me where it's quiet?"

Chrissy looked up at her mother and followed her up to a room that slept four girls with a pair of bunk beds and a fold-up cot. She moved aside her birthday gifts, a diary and a "Chrissy" doll, on her bed. Emily sat next to her on the bed and pulled a quilt across their laps.

"I want to tell you a love story."

Chrissy, young but understanding, knew some of her mother's life. She knew she'd been considered incurable, that she wasn't supposed to end up with a house full of children.

"Does it have a happy ending, Mum?" Chrissy laid her head next to her mother's on the pillow, anxious to hear the story. It wasn't often they had time for just the two of them. Her mother stroked the soft golden waves, the same color as her own.

"It sure does, Sweetheart."

EPILOGUE

From early childhood, I have heard stories of my mother's experiences in the state TB preventatorium for children. She spoke about the friends she made there—many of whom died at early ages—and the sadness, fear, and hopelessness she often felt as one treatment after another failed to improve her condition. She said the two things that kept her going during those dark days were faith in God and the love of her sweetheart, Len.

I am so thankful that Mother instilled a love of God in me, because I regularly look to Him for guidance when I am struggling with a problem. Invariably, the answer comes and I thank God again for His ever-present love and watchfulness over all of us. In fact, it was God who led me to write this book. I felt Him telling me that too many people are suffering and they need to hear a story about the power of His love. I look around, and all I see is a nation that is hurting. I wrote this book to help families who are enduring hardships to face their troubles and conquer them with full trust, hope, and faith in God.

My father, Len, has been a steadfast presence in my life, and has been there for my mother ever since they met and fell in love. He never lost faith that she would be well enough to marry him, and he always believed they would have the family they so dearly wanted. When my mother was ill, Dad was always there by her side. She was the love of his life, just as he was the same to her. This book has special meaning for him, and he has participated in its birth and evolution all the way to final publication. Thank you, Dad, for your constant love and support.

My parents taught me that a simpler way of living is the key to happiness!

ABOUT THE AUTHOR

The author with her father

Chris Carpenter was born and raised in beautiful Johnstown, Pennsylvania. She met her husband, Joe, at a wedding. She asked him to dance, and they have been dancing through life ever since.

They have four wonderful children and a granddaughter.

Chris has always enjoyed journaling and all of the arts. Most of all, she loves people and hearing their true stories.

She hears God's voice and knows the time is now for this incredible story to be shared with the world.

Contact the author at cfcarpenter9@gmail.com to share your true story.